Inherit the Land

Landowners in the 'Eighties

Inherit

LAWRENCE RICH

the Land
Landowners in the 'Eighties

An introduction by the Duke of Grafton

Photographs by Martin Trelawny

UNWIN HYMAN
London   Sydney

To the many families whose fortune has been to
inherit important country houses and landed estates,
and who have risen to the challenge of steering
them unscathed through the rocks of the 'Eighties,
this modest book is dedicated.

First published in Great Britain by Unwin
Hyman, an imprint of Unwin Hyman
Limited, 1987

UNWIN HYMAN LIMITED
Denmark House,
37–39 Queen Elizabeth Street
London SE1 2QB
and
40 Museum Street, London WC1A 1LU

Allen & Unwin Australia Pty Ltd
8 Napier Street, North Sydney,
NSW 2060, Australia

Allen & Unwin New Zealand Ltd
with the Port Nicholson Press
60 Cambridge Terrace, Wellington,
New Zealand

ISBN 0 04 440052 7

Cataloguing in Publication Data

Inherit the land: landowners in the eighties.
1. Landowners—Great Britain—
Interviews
333.3'0941   HD598

Designed by Norman Reynolds

Printed and bound in Italy

Contents

Introduction by the Duke of Grafton KG
6

Preface
8

Longleat, Wiltshire:
The Marquess of Bath
12

Slane Castle, County Meath:
The Earl of Mount Charles
36

Littlecote, Wiltshire:
Peter de Savary, Esquire
58

Achnacarry, Inverness-shire:
Sir Donald Cameron of Lochiel
76

Ebberston Hall, North Yorkshire:
West de Wend Fenton, Esquire
106

Hall Place, Kent:
The Lord Hollenden
122

Sark, Channel Islands:
Michael Beaumont, Esquire, the Seigneur of Sark
140

Beaulieu, Hampshire:
Lord Montagu of Beaulieu
164

Introduction

by the Duke of Grafton KG

I have always felt that a very dramatic book could be written about landowning in the UK (and this book includes Eire as well), and this Lawrence Rich has now done. I was only 17 when my father unexpectedly inherited the Euston Estate in Suffolk, which was then in a state of near-bankruptcy and faced a crippling bill for death duties, and I was quickly made conscious of the appalling problems which accompany the owner-ship of estates, large houses and collections. My father surmounted them, but only just, and everything was very nearly sold in 1938.

It is perhaps this experience which led me, after the War, into the heritage lobby, which has done such invaluable work for the preservation of historic houses and estates. I have been chairman of the SPAB for over 20 years, started by William Morris in 1877. He can have had little idea that his violent campaign against what he called 'conjectural restoration' of historic buildings would turn into a pressure group concerned with the preservation of some of the most important buildings in the country. I have worked for the National Trust both as a regional representative and, for 15 years, as chairman of the Trust's East Anglian regional committee, and I am still a member of the properties committee.

Since its inception in 1953, I have served on the Historic Buildings Council for England, which has now been absorbed by the Historic Buildings and Monuments Commission, and I still serve as a member of its Historic Buildings Advisory Committee. In my 31 years as a member of the HBC, I have had an unrivalled opportunity to study the problems of the landed estate owner with a valuable house, and like to think that the council has been able to save a great many historic houses with vitally important grants, and is continuing to do so.

When the threat of a wealth tax seemed imminent in 1976, so endangering Britain's heritage, I became involved in the formation of the Historic Houses Association. As a comparatively new but formidable body the Association has achieved legislative marvels. Among their achievements was the organization of a giant petition to Parliament signed by over a million people visiting historic houses, pressing for legislation to save the heritage.

All these jobs have given me invaluable experience of these highly complex matters. The solution to the problem will never be complete. What is certain is that it is the devotion of the owners to their estates which has preserved them so far, and I am delighted to have been asked to write the introduction to such an absorbing story, told by so expert and varied a group of owners.

Grafton

Preface

*I*n Britain, there is a greater wealth of country houses than anywhere else in the world, surviving intact with their treasures and landed estates. Apart from her poetry, Britain's greatest contribution to the arts has unquestionably been the country house. Far more than just the bricks and mortar, this term embraces the gardens and landscaped parks, and the woods and fields. It covers the ancillary buildings clustered around the stable- and estate-yards: the dairy, laundry, dovecote and ice-house; the saw-mill, the carpenter's shop, brew-house (cider press in the West Country) and forge; the skinloft where buckskin was cured and dressed; the Home Farm whose produce supported household and retainers; the kennels, stables, coach-house and tack room, and all the buildings both fanciful and functional which are part of the formal and kitchen gardens.

For centuries, many great houses were more village than family dwellings. What we mean by 'country house life' applies to attitudes and a way of life reaching beyond the walls of the house itself. Sport has always played an important role. It forged a bond between men watching hounds draw the same coverts, or those who thread the same bog in pursuit of snipe. This bond, as every sportsman knows, extends to hunt servants, gamekeepers and loaders alike reviving some primeval survival factor whose appeal is shared by all participants. In the same way, country house life extends to the estate's lesser houses and craftsman-built cottages (no less architecturally and sociologically important), and to the community which has traditionally both supported and been supported by the entire complex. These communities can be equated to a modern company in which the landowner serves as chairman, while the host of individuals from steward to pantry boy, head gardener to hedger, may be regarded as shareholders in the joint endeavour. Of course, ultimately it was up to the family, and its ability to ride fences both political and economic, to ensure the continuity and well-being of the community.

At Knole in Kent – a substantial household – 90 servants would regularly eat together in the Great Hall. Many families, such as the Yorkes of Erddig, in Clywd, North Wales, related to their servants and estate workers with a warmth that our 20th-century employers of fleeting *au pairs* might regard with incredulity. They embraced them as it were, as part of their extended family. The Yorkes had portraits painted of generations of retainers (and latterly photographed), which they framed and hung on their walls. They wrote verses to commemorate their idiosyncracies. They laughed with them, indulged them, despaired of or admired them. In a word, they loved them as part and parcel of their own lives. By the same token the servants in unnumbered country houses loved and revered the houses they were attached to, and the families with those destinies they were inextricably bound up. When the National Trust accepted Arlington Court in Devon, and later Anglesey Abbey near Cambridge, the men who stepped forward to become those properties' administrators were not retired Brigadiers or ex-Colonial administrators but the butlers who had worked for their donors. When in the Trust's employment, the former butler of Arlington Court would reminisce about opulent shooting parties and he described how he cleared the rooms first thing in the morning relishing the aroma of cigars enjoyed the night before by 'the toffs'. At Anglesey Abbey, the butler – who rejoiced in the most apposite names of Grimes – was, however, to be driven to the verge of paranoia. It was Grimes' nightmare that the public, eager to enjoy his Abbey's art treasures, would troop across his beloved carpets without first scraping the fenland from their feet.

France and Italy may have richer architectural heritages. All too often, however, their *chateaux* and *palazzi*, bereft of furniture, survive as little more than beautiful but empty shells. Britain, by contrast, has been immensely fortunate. Many houses contain collections of fine furniture, paintings and textiles which have been steadily built up over the generations for hundreds of years. No enemy since the Norman Conquest has made it across the Channel to sack our homes and even the spirited attempts of the tax-man have been largely circumvented by communal commonsense laced with native adaptability. In turn each of these have been nutured by an insular instinct to close ranks in the face of threat.

Primogeniture, allied to insularity (in the sense that a finite coastline sets a limit on growth), have also gone a long way to help enrich Britain since younger sons sought their fortunes overseas. From the corners of the earth, trees and plants were shipped back to adorn the gardens; pictures, statuary, furniture and ceramics, silverware, arms and armour from the East, the New World, the colonies and Empire – all were sent to grace a thousand British homes. The pensions, savings and fortunes of these sons enabled them to stake a claim on the soil of Home and create the sort of establishment they regarded as appropriate.

It is truism that the English country house has always been accessible to the interested public. Jane Austen writes of visiting Chatsworth. Sarah, Duchess of Malborough, complained bitterly of the Oxford populace scrambling over Blenheim Palace before its completion. Horace Walpole, in the 18th century, was incapable of resisting a pair of gate piers if the drive beyond them led to an unvisited mansion. At Wilton House, Wiltshire, in 1776, 2,324 people had been shown round before August, each tipping the housekeeper 2s 6d. This, 'open house' tradition harks back to medieval – even Saxon – times, the lord and his people holding together against intruders. In a number of ways the great house served – and serves – as a rallying point, a community emblem, a focus of local pride. It may be visited because one's grandmother worked there as a maid, or one's great uncle as an under-gardener. It may be visited for its craftmanship in masonry, joinery, cabinet-making or plasterwork. It attracts many for its art collections, for its ancient power, its endurance, and its place in our rolling island history. It may be visited for its blend of woodsmoke, *pot pourri* and beeswax and for the whiff these supply of civilized comfort . . . and a country house may also be visited out of a desire to see how the other half lived.

In the last decade of Queen Victoria's reign, a charity was founded to preserve 'places of historic interest and natural beauty' for the enjoyment of that and future generations. This was the National Trust, now the foremost conservation society in the land. For the first half of its life the Trust concentrated on bringing coast and countryside under its protective wing. In doing so, it inevitably became the owner of farms and cottages and ancillary buildings – and by the mid-30s, also of a handful of more substantial, if mainly empty, buildings – Bodiam Castle, Sussex, the Bath Assembly Rooms, and Montacute House in Somerset. Towards the end of the decade, however, it became plain that the entity called the 'country house' was under threat from unprecedented pressures. Personal taxation – death duties in particular – were so rapidly undermining the fortunes of the rich that within a couple of generations the achievement, which had sometimes taken centuries to perfect, could well become as extinct as the mastadon. Accordingly, the Trust adapted to the challenge and in 1941 accepted Blickling Hall in Norfolk as its first country house complete with setting and historic contents. The bequest also included an agricultural and woodland estate of 4,767 acres, 25 farms, 137 houses and cottages, a pub and several other lesser buildings. Less than 50 years on, the historic houses that they have been accepted by the Trust now number close on 90.

This phenomenon is remarkably British. Few other people would willingly pass to an independent charity their ancestral home with its accumulated contents, its land and a substantial slice of the family fortune as an endowment for future upkeep. Yet this has been the case with scores of families. They have gladly entrusted their properties to the National Trust.

Fortunately, the five decades since the acquisition of Blicking have seen country house visiting become a major leisure activity. Arising from this, and the drain of art treasures, have come more enlightened fiscal measures making it easier for the private owner of 'heritage' property to keep it watertight and prevent its break up. Opening to the public on a regular basis, and providing additional attractions to maximize revenue, is a form of diversification open to many country house owners. Other owners choose to arrange sporting lets, holiday cottages, farming partnerships or salmon hatcheries. Today in Britain, no great house can support itself, as before the War, on the income it derives solely from agriculture. The need to adapt is nothing new to the British – although the areas into which this takes some landowners today might be looked on as opportunist, demeaning or downright vulgar. Yet the only true yardstick to judge them against is the measure of security they provide for the land and all it contains, and the security it gives to both landowner and tenant, as well as the families of each of these. The fundamentals do not change. Today – as in the past, and no doubt in the years ahead – interdependence is the core ingredient for making a living from a heritage property while keeping those aspects alive which are essential to its character.

Longleat

Longleat

Wiltshire:
The Marquess of Bath

*T*hread the narrow lanes along the Wiltshire-Somerset border, and there comes a point where you are overtaken by expectancy. You are within the orbit of a great country house. Although screened by farmland and belts of timber, the house and its occupants betray themselves by a cohesion in the landscape. The signs are in its hedgerows, in its farm buildings and cottages, and in the ratios of pasture, plough and woodland. Above all, the effects of sympathetic long-term management are seen in the way that the timber is managed and disposed of with profitability tempered by respect for landscape.

Approached from Warminster, Longleat is heralded by the 800ft bulk of Cley Hill. Three decades ago this dominating landscape and archaeological feature was presented by the fifth Marquess of Bath to the National Trust. The Iron Age ramparts that encircle its crown command the plain below and some 10,000 acres owned by the family which has held power here since Tudor times. Skirting Cley Hill, the road shortly lands you at a minor junction, and on the right opens the entrance to a modest private drive. Once through the gate, however, and into the woodland beyond, any ideas about modesty must be instantly up-graded. The arboretum laid out about the carriageway displays a plantsman's flair backed by dedicated management. It provides an open-air exhibition of exotic trees and flowering shrubs – a 20th-century creation, already mature, against the backdrop of working forestry.

For a mile this achievement of colour, form and texture runs along both sides of the drive. As light glances through from the right the landscaper's sleight of hand is revealed, however, for the designer's skill has, indeed, quite literally made one miss the wood for the trees. Manicured shrubs and specimen trees have conspired, with their backdrop, to withold attention from the feat of topography developing behind their screen. While the carriageway has been proudly showing off the arboretum, the ground out of sight has swept away down a boldly plunging escarpment; and when the drive emerges from a stand of beeches, it lands you on the lip of Salisbury Plain to be bowled over by the breathtaking view below. Landscape designers from 'Capability' Brown to Humphrey Repton have risen to the challenge. Few indeed could resist trying to improve on this site and the potential presented by its broad and moving canvas. In some old prints the viewpoint appears under the title Prospect Hill. Its name today is no less appropriate. You are standing at Heaven's Gate.

While the beech trees pursue the ridge at Heaven's Gate and the driveway snakes down the escarpment, you look down over an undulating sea of grass that laps almost to the walls of the Elizabethan palace far below glittering in the sun a full half mile away. Beyond, and on either side, the Somerset plain rolls to the dim blue distance.

The scale of the place is so stupendous, the site so overpowering, that preconceptions may well have to be adjusted. These beech trees were planned by 'Capability' Brown some 230 years ago and the house on the plain below dates from two centuries earlier. But besides its historical weight, the place is significant for a number of reasons which are in some danger of being overlooked. For isn't this the seat of the 'Mad' Marquess

Safari boat on a quest for sea lions and hippopotomi.

of Bath, the originator of stately home razzmatazz? So where, one might ask, is the vulgarity, the Blackpool atmosphere? Where the paper bags and fish and chips?

Down on the grassland rock-grey lumps might just be identified as rhinos. And on Half-Mile Pond beyond, a 'safari boat' chugs through the haunt of sea-lions and hippopotami and noses round Humphrey Repton's island peopled today by gorillas. So broad is the sweep that neither animals nor visitors appear obtrusive, and the principal star unquestionably remains the house. Longleat – England's earliest and most splendid Renaissance country house – stands centre-stage, dominating the scene with all its economic, social, aesthetic, artistic and – pre-eminently – historical connotations.

The most revolutionary period in England's history was not, as its name might suggest, the Civil War of the 17th century but rather, in terms of the structure of Britain's society, the Tudor dynasty followed by the effects of World War One. The former gave rise to the creation of Longleat. The latter almost led to its destruction. It is not easy to appreciate the surge of relief which greeted the end of the Wars of the Roses. Richard III was toppled in 1586 on the horseless field of Bosworth, and his defeat brought the Tudors to power, letting the rude Middle Ages roll into history. Central government was tightened. Trade and commerce received their new green light. With the lifting of the threat of strife, our ancestors could at last hang up their weapons in the confidence that their castle could equally be a home. Within a generation, lofty mullioned windows were punched through in place of arrow slits, gardens blossomed in the moat, walls were panelled in oak or draped with tapestries to bring warmth and colour to cold stone rooms. Then followed the master-stroke – Henry VIII's break with Rome. Whatever his motives – a complex mixture of personal, political and fiscal desires – the important fact is that, as a by-product of his Dissolution, the wealth of a thousand abbeys and other religious houses was thrown on the market – farmland, woodland, fishing and industrial interests – with the capital investment they represented and their incomes in terms of rents and tithes. While the Church of England was established out of those abbeys which were ready to accept the change (together with a handful of newly-created sees), the monastic complexes dissolved by the king were either sold or handed out among his supporters as bribes, or as rewards for services rendered. Not far from Longleat, across the fields, it is said that Little Jack Horner (one of the new men with a finger in the pie) pulled out his exceptionally covetable plum – the abbey of Mells with its supporting manors. At Longleat, meanwhile, where the old priory mill was distinguished by its long 'leat', or tail-race, a certain John Thynne paid £53 for a ruinous monastic building with its tumbledown mill and 60 acres of orchard and warren. The year was 1540. Thynne was 25 years old.

Ambitious greedy, not noted for scruples, John Thynne displayed financial shrewdness, quick-footed agility on the political tightrope, and seemingly boundless energy. Longleat, his bold and prodigious building, reveals, too, his appreciation of quality and his firm artistic grasp. Thynne's tastes were remarkably ahead of his time: England's country-side had seen nothing quite like it before for the house ante-dates those other great Elizabethan palaces – Hardwick Hall, Wollaton and Burghley.

John Thynne, 'The Builder', was the son of a Shropshire squire. At an early age he worked in London as a kitchen clerk to his uncle William Thynne, chief clerk to Henry VIII's royal kitchens. But with a sharp eye on advancement young Thynne quickly progressed to the household of the Earl of Hertford – Edward Seymour, brother of the king's wife Jane Seymour, and thus uncle of their wretched and sickly son who was to reign briefly as Edward VI. Among Seymour's lucrative responsibilities was the disposal of confiscated monastic properties, clearly a field wide open to abuse. There can be little doubt that his protégé, John Thynne, was quick to cash in on any pickings to be had.

In 1547 Henry VIII died, and during the ensuing minority of Edward VI, Seymour (now Duke of Somerset), became his nephew's guardian and the most powerful man in the realm. This was a good time for Thynne. Elsewhere in the West Country he amassed church manors scattered across five counties from Dorset to Shropshire – rich revenue-producing meadows, orchards, deer parks and woods, and the wheat-lands and sheep-walks that would support his dynasty. By the time he was knighted at 36, he had extended Longleat from 60 to 6,000 acres. He was not much liked, and not greatly trusted, but Sir John Thynne was certainly acknowledged to be rich. It had taken him a bare eleven years.

Subsequent Thynnes were a mixed bag. Connoisseurs sired scoundrels, drunkards followed bibliophiles, spendthrifts alternated with men of financial rectitude. One is said to have killed his wife's lover (a skeleton wearing top-boots, unearthed in the cellars, lends macabre substance to this story); another was assassinated; and a third ran off with and married a toll-keeper's daughter. Yet the long-term graph of the Thynne family fortunes shows the persistent rise of a business under sound management control. More marriages were judicious than disastrous, more landed estates were acquired than squandered. In 1682 the sixth lord of Longleat was elevated to the peerage as Viscount Weymouth; the eighth, in 1798, became Marquess of Bath and received George III and Queen Charlotte.

The Home Farm, reorganized in the 1870s to the most up-to-date standards.

The high-point of prosperity, however was achieved in the palmy days of Queen Victoria when John Alexander Thynne, fourth Marquess of Bath, came into his inheritance in 1852. Thirty years later the Longleat income alone amounted to a staggering £68,000 a year, and the Marquess received further income from other estates – including land in Ireland running to 22,000 acres. During the earlier years of his reign, in particular, the fourth Marquess dutifully reinvested his Longleat profits to finance far-seeing estate improvements. He modernized the Home Farm to the most up-to-date plan and standards, built a foundry, fitted out his properties with new carts and waggons, and bought a new-fangled, steam-driven saw bench and steam plough and other items of the most modern equipment available. Throughout those decades, profitability was assumed to be as unshakeable as the Empire. The winter of 1881 brought the Prince of Wales and Princess Alexandra to Longleat for four days of entertainment and shooting. The bag was over 1,000 birds a day. At this time there were nearly 50 indoor servants, and the estate could muster 20 gamekeepers. In addition to these, there were some 50 woodmen, 30 in the gardens, 50 farmworkers, no less than 14 grooms and coachmen and a further 50 general labourers under the Clerk of Works. (An interesting footnote, in view of today's Safari Park, is that the fourth

The Bath Arms, *Longleat's estate pub in the village of Horningsham.*

Marquess was thought not a little dotty by his fellow Victorians for studying the habits of the kangaroos kept in an enclosure in his pheasantry.)

Yet amid all this settled splendour the wind of change was blowing. Rail transport in the 1870s from the American corn belt brought cheap grain to England. With the advent of refrigeration in the following decade came meat from South America, Australia and New Zealand to cut the market from beneath the British farmer. At the same time, forestry revenue dropped. Who wanted English oak for battleships when a Navy of ironclads maintained the world pink?

Estates like Longleat were hit particularly hard by the 30 year agricultural depression. On the rolling chalk and limestone belts of southern England, for hundreds of years fortunes have been guaranteed for those lucky enough to own land – provided that is, that there has been a market for wool and corn, and for their cattle fattened in the valleys. Many now switched to milk production to satisfy the ever-increasing consumption of the still expanding cities. In the conditions prevailing in the '80s, however, the Marquess of Bath was forced to turn to his Irish estates and to sell when reinvestment was demanded. Part of Bath's trouble had stemmed from his embarking on an ambitious and costly programme of refurbishing the state rooms at Longleat in 1874. This entailed, for example, gutting the 16th-century long gallery and transforming it into the present saloon, with its sumptuous decoration and the French period furniture then the fashion. He went on to duplicate this style throughout the principal rooms in the house.

With the First World War following fast on the agricultural depression, the old prosperity was never fully to return. In need of capital, like his father not 50 years before, the fifth Marquess bit the bullet and disposed of more land – this time 8,600 acres of the Longleat estate itself. Times were never as bad as the dark days between 1919 to 1921. In the five years that followed the Armistice, it is said that as much as a quarter of England changed hands. Lord Bath was fortunate: his sales realized £350,000. True, land values had risen sharply as a result of the War, but while rents remained static, wages had rocketed to three times their pre-1914 level. An ordered way of life that had changed but little for centuries was suddenly and irrevocably altered. Before the War, Longleat had still ticked along on an indoor staff of 43. Domestic service employed more than any other occupation in those days. But after nearly half a million female servants broke their traditional ties to pitch in for the war-effort, only a portion was to return to their former existence. There followed the introduction of electricity – this came to Longleat in 1928 – with its welcome labour-saving advantages. The petrol engine's arrival released grooms and coachmen and foreshadowed an even more startling shedding of labour from the land. Unprecedented levels of income tax were introduced; and then, before the generation was out World War Two was upon the country, to be followed by increased death duties, inflation and world recession. By 1946, when Hitler's War ended, Longleat as it had been, along with a host of other country houses, was bleakly faced with the possibility of extinction.

The pattern of life that had started with the Tudors had finally run its course. All across the land great houses were being shuttered and deserted – or knocked down to give place to smaller homes. Yet the principal threat to that way of life was not so much the hammer of the demolition gang as the mallet of the auctioneer. Family collections of pictures, silver, tapestries, fine furniture, libraries and other works of art – treasures that in many cases had lain cheek-by-jowl for centuries – were sold and dispersed as their owners found themselves unable to adapt to the times.

Henry Frederick Thynne, sixth Marquess of Bath, was 41 years of age and freshly de-mobbed when he inherited in 1946. The dilemma he faced was not so much how but – momentarily – whether he could make a go of it. The twelfth in succession from Sir John Thynne, The Builder, Henry

Tranquility can be savoured in this most elegant of boat-houses.

Nowhere in Horningsham are you out of touch with green fields and trees.

Henry and Virginia Bath.

could be regarded as a man exceptionally favoured by the gods. His inheritance ran to 16,000 acres of prime Wiltshire farmland and woods. He came into one of the most splendid mansions in England. He became the owner of its magnificent treasures, most of them still at that time packed away for the duration in the stables while Longleat housed a girls' school. However, besides these assets Henry also came in for a death duties bill which amounted to a staggering £700,000 – an enormous sum in those days.

It is only because much of the tenacity, boldness and lateral thinking of The Builder had re-emerged in Henry that Longleat was able to survive. In the process of keeping house and estate together, and ensuring its commercial success, Henry Bath pioneered the solution for hundreds of other country houses. All over Britain owners were to follow his lead, and today their properties face the future with a confidence many had not experienced since before the 1870s when the bottom fell out of agriculture.

Before the Second World War Henry had read agriculture at Oxford. To the practical land management experience he had absorbed almost incidentally while growing up on a large estate, were now added the advantages of academic theory. As a young man he had determined that when the estate was his he would do his damnedest to keep it afloat.

Shortage of capital had meant that cottages had been running down and some farms and estate roads neglected. High wages had put paid to the extensive estate staff of former years. The days of 30 gardeners, to take but one area, were decidedly a thing of the past. Henry was well aware that if his family home and the people who depended upon it were to ride the flood tide of the 20th century, he – and they – would have to learn to adapt.

His pre-war efforts had already produced substantial savings. For instance, Henry had set about reducing the formal gardens – putting an end, for example, to the practice of 'bedding out' – in order to cut back on maintenance staff. Other measures adopted were both more ambitious and positive. Henry's great passion has always been woodland management, and the personal care of individual trees. In 1929 he had cleared the woods of 80 years' accumulated undergrowth – mainly rhododendron run wild – introducing in their place new and rarer shrubs, such as those along the drive above Heaven's Gate; and he established extensive new plantations of commercial timber.

After the War and faced with a massive bill for death duties, a run-down estate, and a 118-roomed mansion to house a household comprising of himself, his wife and their four children, Henry had first to concentrate on his debts. Next would come the estate, and then the house. So priority number one was to acquire capital and pay off the bills. Secondly he would restore the estate to good heart. Only then could he expect to gain a return from his inheritance.

Towards defraying the death duties bill he sold 4,500 acres. Then he looked at the farms. Many of these were ripe for reorganization. Traditionally they had been held 'in hand', that is, farmed by the estate for the profit of the estate and employing labour which was housed on the estate. Henry's policy was to rent his farms to tenants. This was perhaps no more than the responsible action of any good landowner who felt it his duty to try to keep the community buoyant. But it was an arrangement that took some of the burden off his own shoulders while providing employment and a stronger profit incentive to the families which – as much as the Thynnes themselves – had for generations depended on that very land. As tenancies fell in, therefore, Lord Bath reorganized the holdings to create more economic units. At the same time, he pursued a programme of reconstructing farm buildings many of which had barely been touched since Victorian times. In his first ten years, he spent more than £300,000 on providing up-to-date machine sheds, storage and animal houses so that his farms could at least compete in the 20th century.

RIGHT: *Peacocks in Paradise.*

Meanwhile, his beloved woods were in urgent need of attention. With the assistance of 250 German prisoners-of-war he quickly cleared and re-planted 150 acres of woodland that had been requisitioned and clear-felled in the War. In other parts of the estate were a wartime American hospital and an RAF depot. Both had to be tackled. Huts were demolished, concrete roads ripped up and removed, and all requisitioned land reabsorbed. Within four years of taking over, Henry also felled the elms that flanked the three-quarter mile drive from South Lodge to the house, and replaced them with four lines of tulip trees.

With these measures behind him he could now direct attention on the house, and on the gardens that were still draining him of some £30,000 a year. More essential in the present circumstances, Henry felt, would be the input of one intelligent and practical carpenter than the butler, two odd-job men, one lad, the housekeeper, three housemaids, three laundry maids, the cook and two motor men who had staffed the house in 1939. Longleat had been standing for four centuries. During its first 300 years it had been maintained by a succession of skilled craftsmen. In the fourth it had been left largely to fend for itself since his grandfather's moderniz-ation of the 1870s. Two massive stone chimneys were now in danger of collapse, and the roof itself demanded immediate attention. Death watch beetle, reducing the main timbers to powder, was cohabiting with both wet-rot and dry-rot, and they were pressing home their three-pronged attack on the fabric. Further horrors, clearly, would reveal themselves once panelling and floorboards and ceilings were removed and a proper assessment of the problems made.

While it is true that many great houses in private hands have long been accessible to visitors, their opening on the scale we know today was unthinkable in the mid-40s. Even the National Trust, which now opens 180 or more houses to the public, did not embark on its 'Country House Scheme' until 1941 when it was given its first historic house complete with contents and historic setting. For this reason Henry Bath's decision in the spring of 1948 to restore his home to its pre-war condition, and to open it regularly to the public as a commercial enterprise, was greeted with incredulity by both the press and his peers. It was forecast that nobody would come. Petrol was still rationed. No restoration grants were available. The public, it was predicted, would steal his possessions. They would trample his gardens to destruction. In a word, life would be made intolerable. Henry was popularly dubbed the 'Mad' Marquess of Bath. But he was encouraged by the way his Cheddar Caves, nearby, steadily attracted large numbers of visitors. And like The Builder before him, he was blessed with energy and vision. If there was madness in his

The Orangery.

method, then his lapse from sanity was amply offset by method in his madness.

First the lead was lifted from the roof, and the ancient timbers repaired. Furniture was brought in from the stables and outbuildings to be returned to their former positions. Many items were unhappily found to be badly distressed from their long sentence in the stables. It had been a good war for moths. A party of devoted Bristol nuns tirelessly revived tapestries and needlework that had suffered from their voracious attention. The house came alive again – throughout the months it was the scene of carpenters, French polishers, picture restorers, glaziers, cabinet-makers, upholsterers, designers and decorators. More than £80,000 was poured in to the property to counter the ravages of death watch beetle, and on insecticide treatment. The fifth Marquess's war-time ground floor bedroom was converted into a souvenir shop. Silver was uncrated and polished for display on the state room tables. The fifth Marchioness's clothes, with her hats and parasols, emerged from tissue-paper wrapping to form a special display of their own. The 18th-century stage coach received a face-lift. New gardens were laid out, paths widened, lavatories installed and car parking provided. Then one day in April 1949, with Henry standing on the steps in welcome, the first paying visitors to Longleat ventured up the drive. They were marshalled in the car park by Viscount Weymouth, Henry's oldest son and heir, and they bought their tickets to wander through the rooms of a great and aristocratic private house. On that day a new leisure activity was born. They have been coming to Longleat ever since.

The first opening season saw 135,000 visitors who paid 2s 6d each. Their half-crowns grossed nearly £17,000 for the house and estate. An exceptional year nowadays (with a year-round season excepting only Christmas day) can yield as many as 300,000 visitors, with the average hovering somewhere around the 220,000 mark.

The first private house to open regularly to visitors, Longleat was also the first to offer a 'safari park'. This resulted from an approach by the circus promoter Jimmy Chipperfield in 1964. He suggested that animals should be maintained in the park and be made a special pubic attraction. 'I didn't quite understand at first what he was driving at,' Henry recalls. 'The fact is, I'm not particularly fond of animals – except cats and dogs or course . . .' The animals which Chipperfield had in mind were not cats or dogs: they were lions. He also made the proposal – bizarre at the time – that whereas the lions should roam free within their extensive enclosures, the public should view them, as it were, caged in their cars.

The deal they struck was that Henry should pay for the fences and roads

The steps up to the entrance to Longleat House make a valuable resting place.

The Lions of Longleat.

while his partner provided 50 lions and covered the cost of their upkeep. They went into it together on a fifty-fifty basis. Longleat's parkland extends to 700 acres – providing ample room to lay out the complex. In April 1966 the venture opened with an entrance charge of £1 per car. The controversy preceding the opening had ensured 'the Lions of Longleat' wide publicity – so much so that in the event they thoroughly captured public enthusiasm. By the end of that first season the setting up costs had been fully recovered.

Twenty years on, the safari park now embraces a wide variety of animals, and is managed by Roger Cawley, Jimmy Chipperfield's son-in-law. Together with the house itself, it remains the major attraction. These are however only two of eleven or more special features offered by the 'All-in-one Discount Ticket' recently introduced by Lord Christopher Thynne, younger son of Lord Bath. Attractions include a trip on a safari boat, a ride on the miniature Longleat railway, entrance to the Victorian kitchens, the collection of dolls' houses, the BBC's Dr. Who Exhibition, a pets corner, Lord Bath's bygones, and the maze – the biggest in the world – whose labyrinthine complexities were devized by Viscount Weymouth.

Generations of beloved pets in the animals' cemetery behind the house.

Lord Bath, now a vigorous 84, combines urbanity, charm and disarming simplicity. He is, of course, by no means simple. His innovative approach to the salvation of that endangered species, the country house, would itself have earned him a niche in posterity. But on top of all that, he has shown himself to be the country's greatest natural showman. For 40 years he has confounded us all with his boldness, imagination and sense of fun – and his knack of always seeming to detect public taste in advance. Henry's flair for publicity depends not only on his nose for a news story but equally on his organizational ability. Of all qualities, however, perhaps his most outstanding has been his unfeigned understanding and love of people. It is this that has endeared him to those who have met him, and to a far wider public that reaches into every facet of our country. Henry is known as a man of prodigious energy – as have been many of his forebears. At well over six foot, his bearing and clear eyes announce him every inch a Thynne. Nor does it make a whit of difference that the fine, straight nose – characteristic of generations of Thynnes – has been broken since his youth. It lends a slightly swashbuckling element to the old Marquess's appearance, giving him a rather piratical look with the

'. . . or a ride on Longleat's miniature railway. . .'

The BBC's 'Doctor Who' experience.

Help! Confusion in Viscount Weymouth's maze – the biggest in Europe.

spotted red 'handkerchief' tie he habitually sports. He is a man of easy good humour and unfailing interest in all that goes on in his domain.

Henry Bath runs the house and park with the detailed, day-to-day assistance of Christopher Thynne, his right-hand man. They are backed by a hard-working professional staff. In maintaining this great enterprise, they provide employment for as many local people as were on the Longleat estate's payroll in its past heyday. Alexander Weymouth meanwhile has been given responsibility for the estate. In many respects the management of Longleat can be compared to that of a large commercial company in which the two brothers represent heads of departments. Henry still retains his old devotion for his trees. Only last year, indeed, he tackled a formerly neglected area of semi-woodland close to the park's Horningsham entrance. Here he personally cleared the scrub and put in hundreds of new trees. At times, too, he may still be seen in the woods, marking timber to be extracted and planning future crops, although obviously he no longer has an aptitude for the heavier aspects of forestry management.

This being so, however, one thing is for sure: Henry Frederick Thynne, sixth Marquess of Bath, still has the ability to come up with something new. He has shown the world that, even in these days, a great house can be made to pay its way. He has shown hundreds of other owners how to make a fist of presentation. And he has brought enjoyment to untold millions of people who might otherwise never have visited a stately home nor set foot in a landscaped park. Furthermore, Henry Bath has paid off death duty bills that might well have driven most others to despair. He has set an example which many have followed but few have succeeded so well.

Close to the house, an area of exotic trees still managed personally by the Marquess of Bath.

Slane Castle

Slane Castle

County Meath:
The Earl of Mount Charles

*I*n 1821, when making his State Visit to Ireland, George IV and his entourage trundled north along the 30-mile 'Straight Road' which still leaves Dublin today. Slicing across country as uncompromisingly as a ruler, this highway (now part of the A1 to Belfast) hastens through flattish, undemanding landscape until it swoops into the valley of the river Boyne. From the stone bridge that spans the river, Slane Castle can be seen perched on its hill a mile or so away on the opposite side. The Straight Road was very probably made for this royal occasion when George visited Ireland – one of his first major public duties as king. Although he had been crowned only the year before, a decade had elapsed since his father's madness had led to his appointment as Prince Regent and from 1810 this fashionable, pleasure-loving and extravagant man had held court during the Regency. Those same ten years had also been punctuated with a formidable succession of royal mistresses; and it was the last of these, now the first Marchioness Conyngham, whom the King was going to visit.

The existing Slane Castle dates from the 1780s. It stands on a bluff above a great loop in the Boyne, one of the most emotive rivers in Ireland. The Boyne sweeps round this bluff and then flattens and broadens to spill over a low weir within earshot of the castle. There is a hillside of ancient, hanging trees on one bank and on the other, rough grazing spreads generously on the flood-plain. This is a prospect that smacks of 'Capability' Brown who was commissioned to lay out both the parkland and stables. He never visited Slane, however, but working from plans and sketches he was able to produce his characteristic effect of a landscape ennobled through an arranged marriage of art and nature.

The first Marquess Conyngham's marriage had not been arranged.

But it was judicious and, in view of his wife's long liaison with the King, suprisingly successful. Elizabeth, daughter of a wealthy English wool merchant, was a renowned beauty. Her portrait in the castle by Sir Thomas Lawrence, painted in 1820, may well not be as idealized as are the subjects of many of his other works. Although waspishly dubbed the 'Vice Queen' at Court, even her detractors – and there were several – could not deny her physical attractions. Metternich's mistress, Princess Lieven, says of her that she 'had not an idea in her head . . . nothing but a hand to accept pearls and diamonds with, and an enormous balcony to wear them on'. Elizabeth Conyngham was no dumb blond though. A supporter of Catholic emancipation, and strongly opposed to the death penalty, she was also recognized as a useful moderating influence on George IV. However, at the same time she contrived to influence him in favour of her family; and we are told by a contemporary diarist that the King was as devoted to her son Francis Nathaniel 'as if he were his own son – probably a good deal more so'.

As second Marquess, Francis Nathaniel was to achieve success both at Court, where he served as Lord Chamberlain to William IV and later Queen Victoria, and by attaining Cabinet rank in politics. He married the daughter of the first Marquess of Anglesey – the redoutable 'Old One Leg' – who, as Lord George Paget, had commanded Wellington's cavalry at Waterloo with such dash and near disaster. At the close of that

Less forbidding than the castle itself, Slane's stable block has an intimate charm.

battle, while riding off the field at the side of the Duke, Paget's right leg was smashed by a random charge of grapeshot. The Duke of Wellington was watching the routed enemy. 'My God sir,' Paget is said to have uttered, 'I've lost my leg.' Wellington, momentarily removing the spyglass from his eye, glanced down to reply, 'My God sir, so you have,' then calmly resumed his scrutiny of the fleeing French.

The seventh Marquess Conyngham, present head of the family, lives on the Isle of Man. Slane Castle, with its landed estate disposed on both sides of the Boyne, is run by his oldest son and heir to the title – Henry, the Earl of Mount Charles.

Henry was born at Slane. 'I came back from England and a career in publishing to manage 1,000, not very productive, acres. That was ten years ago. I was 25. It would have cost a fortune to maintain the castle as it had been; and although anything approaching this acreage must be considered large for Ireland, since many of the great estates were split up in the last century, I was faced with the impossible equation of maintaining an expensive house on the comparatively meagre income to be derived from farming on its land.'

The seventh Marquess had at one stage actually considered selling the property. 'My father,' Henry Mount Charles admits with candour, 'is now a tax exile.' On the one hand, he explains, Ireland's coalition government had introduced a wealth tax, while on the other it provided only negligible assistance to those with land trying to improve their assets. Henry has a great deal of sympathy for the decisions that were forced upon his father. 'A lot of these revolved around the antagonistic tax régime in this country at the time. Obviously, my father was on the horns of a dilemma. The paradox he faced was quite absurd. It boiled down to the simple yet unavoidable fact that unless he moved out of Ireland there was no possibility of his holding on to Slane. Yet although he wasn't born here, Slane has always been a feature of his life, been part of his psyche since his earliest years. And the decisions he took were probably the right ones. Once taken, they served to relieve him of the management of this and other assets which I've ultimately become involved with; and ultimately these have provided income which has ultimately helped to support this place. It's a sort of continuing circle.'

The two main lines Henry has pursued have been his agricultural operations and those in catering and promotion. 'It was clear,' he recalls, 'that the land in 1976 was vulnerable to wealth tax, was under-performing, and that its farming income could in no way support the

RIGHT: Saints and sinners – a forgotten bishop watches by the Night Club entrance.

estate. At the same time it was both an asset and a liability. The solution had to lie in expanding the asset base and cutting back on the liabilities. This has been my aim over the past ten years.' He has also, as recently as March 1986, been left an adjoining property under the will of a distant kinsman. Beau Parc's 458 acres run contiguous to Slane's and are spread mainly on the high ground across the river from the castle. Beau Parc embraces woodland and some excellent pasture. The bonus which Henry Mount Charles has received, however, is much more than just a chunk of extra land. For where the deep green woods drop suddenly to the Boyne stands a ravishingly beautiful, 18th-century house. Beau Parc itself is a romantic's dream on one of the finest natural sites in Europe. If Henry's ten-year programme of setting the Slane estate on its feet has demonstrated his determination and entrepreneurial skills, the inheritance of an alternative mansion, together with half as much land again, demonstrates a quality even more essential for success: luck.

'First, of course, I took a hard look at the farming side. Benefits from the EEC, in 1976, promised a sound financial base . . . on paper. Encouraged by the bankers, only too anxious to make loans for capital improvements, I investigated setting up a dairy enterprise on what we call Rock Farm – that's the 200 acres directly across the river there which my father bought back when he inherited. Thank heavens I thought better of that venture! If I had done what was suggested, all our assets

Henry, the Earl of Mount Charles.

would have been tied up in milk, and clearly it would have been sheer folly to have got ourselves locked in on a single non-flexible business like that. To my mind the solution lay in flexibility. This I saw in terms of introducing new revenue-producing activities from outside the estate. In Ireland we're paying back 15 per cent interest. You can't manage a business on loans. So as the property needed immediate capital, I raised it instead through the sale of a largely unproductive parcel comprising 16.5 acres on the edge of an existing quarrying concern. It made a gratifying £5,000 an acre. This was a godsend. Irish land prices were depressed, and still are . . . and incidentally look to get worse. Ten years ago you could count on say £4,000 an acre, whereas now you'd be lucky to get £1,200 or even £1,000. We may yet see land tumbling to around £700 an acre.'

Slane had been an agricultural holding by tradition, and it still employed an agricultural staff numbering a manager and 11 workers when Henry took over the estate in 1976. It was natural then that he should move into store cattle – 'that's buying and fattening calves to sell as finished animals at from two to two and a half.' This operation continues, despite the current steep down-turn in cattle prices and recent severe fodder shortages. 'We're aiming at a production level of 200 beasts per season. At the moment I've got 50 mainly Friesian calves and 150 yearlings out there. But to conserve fodder I shall have to sell off a

'At the moment I've got 50 mainly Friesian calves and 150 yearlings out there.'

100 forward stores this season. By this, I mean selling them before they are ready. In their place I hope to take in about 40 calves to be ready to go back into the market in February.'

This is a delicate balancing act. It entails producing if you can – or, if you can't, then buying-in – sufficient foodstuffs to fatten up beasts which will sell at a profit at their optimum weight. Fundamentally, this means producing silage for your older stock, hay for the calves, and a supply of straw for litter. As a rule of thumb, one bullock will consume about five tons of finished silage a year, and on top of that you have your bedding calves. 'With well under 1,000 agricultural acres to play with, and much of that poor by English standards, I can't possibly always remain self-sufficient.' Although Henry reckons to be cutting enough of his own grass to fulfill next winter's silage requirement, he had to buy in 1,500 bales of hay in 1986. 'Last winter we got caught. Normally we're absolutely bang on. But we had two seasons running of diabolical weather and frankly sailed a bit close to the wind. I have been in excess of £10,000 for my feeding costs. It was a salutary lesson learned, and as a result there's no way now that we're not going to come out with a surplus. And if it's a severe winter we might actually sell fodder as cash crop. In the west of Ireland – even parts of this area – people were selling silage at £25 to £30 a ton.'

Henry also maintains about 70 acres under tillage. Mainly barley, this goes to local farmers or the grain cooperative. 'To be realistic, though,' he sums up, 'while traditionally the land has supported the castle, this cannot possibly be the case today. My aim must instead be to enable the estate in its totality – the total resource if you like – to pay for itself through a variety of interlocking enterprises. There may be still a long way to go – but already, financially, the castle is pulling more weight than the land.'

It was very soon after his return to Slane that Henry came to the decision to diversify. From the outset, however, he had one fixed and overriding philosophy: that however hard it would be – and quite obviously there would be sacrifices to be made – he would not move out of Slane, which his family had owned since 1703.

There persists in Ireland a deep and abiding sadness in the impossibility of an absorbtion of the English into Ireland. History clearly shows how any possible warmth could be extinguished. Land was taken over first by the Normans, and later by English and Scottish settlers, then in the 1540s Henry VIII attempted to infiltrate the country with 'responsible' English, and during his daughter Elizabeth's reign the best Irish lands fell into English hands. Their managers treated the Irish with

Gatehouse – to history, or to present-day amusements.

contempt and when Hugh O'Neill (whom Elizabeth made Earl of Tyrone in the hope of winning him over) spearheaded the popular insurrection of 1598, he was eventually deprived of his lands. Further Irish sequestrations by James put some two million acres at the disposal of the Crown, leading to holdings of up to 2,000 acres being apportioned to English and Scottish settlers. Later came Wentworth's appalling behaviour as Deputy in Ireland from 1633, and the events of 1641 when the bitter, frustrated Irish mob slaughtered more than 40,000 Protestants . . . the chronicle is not a pretty one.

The first Conyngham – Alexander – had set up in County Donegal by 1611 – nine years before *The Mayflower* crossed the Atlantic. Originally from western Scotland, he was probably one of those granted land under James I after the flight of Tyrone. In 1690, Alexander's second son, Sir Albert Conyngham, raised a regiment of dragoons for the Protestant King William at the decisive Battle of the Boyne; and his oldest son – later General Henry Conyngham – simultaneously deserted the Catholic Jacobites (supporters of the ousted James II) to swell William III's army with five hundred troops. Thirteen years later, in 1703, this same Henry Conyngham bought the Slane estate on the banks of the very river that had witnessed the Irish and Jacobite armies' defeat by the forces of the new King. Since that year, the family has continuously occupied Slane.

Clearly, today, Slane Castle is an anachronism. Henry Mount Charles' two-sided problem has been how to keep castle and estate intact – and also how to keep the local workforce intact – at the same time as making the place financially sound.

Although the farm staff of eleven has now been reduced to five through natural wastage, Henry's expanding commercial operations have made him the largest employer in the area. An early move was to promote Gus Doggett, his right-hand man, from foreman to farm manager. Not only had Gus's father and grandfather been employed in the gardens at Slane, but his son, too, works for the enterprise as chef in the castle's restaurant set up by Henry. The tradition is important. Where this can be achieved, the present staff enjoy flexible roles in running the complex. Gus Doggett, for example, is equally involved in non-farming enterprises, and as such has taken charge of the hydro-electric plant powered by the Boyne. He also recently rebuilt James Wyatt's castellated, 18th-century park wall where it climbs Mill Hill, the steep approach from the river.

The castle now houses three commercial activities: the restaurant, a night club, and a remarkably profitable reception business. It is rare, on a

Perched on its hill, Slane Castle across the Boyne.

Saturday, not to bump into a wedding party, the happy couple being photographed perhaps against the backdrop of the great grey castle, their friends and relations attacking champagne in the entrance hall, or maybe in the 'Chinese lantern room', and then the whole party – up to a hundred at a time – sitting down to a banquet in the gothic ballroom. This last is a Regency extravaganza and the most elegant room at Slane. It was designed by Thomas Hopper for George IV's visit of 1821. The main hall, pillared and less fanciful, is lined with portraits and is dominated as you enter by the gigantic spread of an Irish elk's horns. The hall is distinguished, too, by a particularly uncompromising quilted bar. 'The aesthetes,' laments Henry, 'the Georgian buffs and so forth, insist on raising the collective eyebrow. But if you're running a catering business you must obviously serve drinks. Anyway,' he concludes, 'the structure's not permanent and can be dismantled at will.'

Even more controversial, in the local mind, have been Henry Mount Charles' ventures into pop festivals. These have been held in the park every year since 1981. Henry aims high. One year it was the Rolling Stones, another Bob Dylan, and Bruce Springsteen in a third. Peaceful these occasions are decidedly not. Nor can it be said that the security fencing, essential for crowd control and an orderly performance, enhances 'Capability' Brown's scheme of things. But these concerts, above all, have kept the wolf from the door and provided capital for further expansion. It costs well in excess of £100,000 to stage one of these Slane shows – 'hundreds of thousands' is Henry's assessment for setting up a one-day event. 'Three days,' he adds, 'I would regard as unmanageable.' By featuring top artists, however, a gate of 70,000 fans can be attracted to the natural amphitheatre below the castle.

So what comes next? Henry has quite a number of projects in mind whose success could depend as much on the buoyancy of the Irish economy as on the cash-flow situation of his estate. His concern, in maximising all the diverse features of the property, is to achieve an acceptable balance between the commercial and the amenity. Besides hydro-electricity, two potential projects are centred on the Boyne itself. Henry is currently looking into the possibilities of bottling and marketing an Irish mineral water; and he is also contemplating a salmon smolt production unit. 'I'm looking for central growth,' he explains, 'All elements should interrelate.' Switching to the profitability of the park, he recalls the Game Fair type of event they recently hosted, and his soundings into the world of three-day events. 'International show jumping should be an absolute natural in horse country like this – and it's certainly more relevant than pop concerts. I find the prospect not unattractive.'

Visitors stroll up to the castle at will.

Henry and Gus Doggett against the backdrop of Mill Hill's hanging woods.

Of his total acreage, some 400 is woodland, and the timber at Slane is being steadily up-graded. While Henry's father put in the spruce plantations in view from the castle, he has recently embarked on underplanting Mill Hill's hanging woods. Over-mature now, from close-to these can be seen to be patchy. He is pursuing a reinstatement programme against the day when the old timber must inevitably go. Meanwhile, he has clear-felled the scrappier elements on the other side of the river, which he will plant up with mixed conifers and hardwoods. Much of this fringe woodland is self-generating, and provides an age mix Henry is anxious to retain. The way in which trees enhance the appearance of the landscape is as important in the long term as their immediate cash value. For this reason here – as elsewhere on the estate – Henry introduces replacement hardwoods when he puts in new commercial conifer blocks, just as he plants up with traditional hardwood species when doing remedial work in distressed areas of timber.

There is also a novel and intriguing cash-crop which Henry Mount Charles is about to try out in a neglected former water-garden area. At present this hollow is notable chiefly for its giant gunnera and its straggle of rather forlorn and waterlogged Sitka. Henry proposes to clear out the scrub and plant it up with ash. 'Quick-growing, and tolerant to wet, there's no reason why commercial ash shouldn't yield a quick return.' In Ireland, ash in saw-log sections has a disproportionate

Softwoods introduced by Henry's father.

value, for it is the main constituent of hurley sticks.

'Roughly a quarter of this place is under trees. I shall have to look into all sorts of woodland activities if I'm to make a financial fist of this resource. I am talking now of forestry, of course; but I am also talking of many other spin-offs and side issues which can be organized from managing woodlands. We must consider how, for instance, we can best exploit the shooting potential . . . perhaps pony trekking . . . nature trails . . . outdoor sports. . . There may well be other applications as well.'

The shooting syndicate arrangements, made by Henry's father, are peculiar to this estate. 'The syndicate shoots ten guns and covers all the costs relating to their sport. They pay for – you name it – the two keepers employed, the rearing of pheasants, the beaters, the insurance. It refunds us, too, for all incidental costs incurred by the estate in regard to the shoot.' If Gus Doggett, to take an example, is called on to organize a tractor to haul birds, then that element is accounted for by the shoot. 'And in return,' smiles Henry, 'I get a gun per day throughout the shoot, plus one day in the year totally mine – a day of my choice which I can either sell for myself or can use to entertain my friends.'

Those who don't know him, put Henry Mount Charles down as a bit of a whizz-kid, a financial manipulator, a man interested primarily in turning a fast buck. But after school he went to Africa, where he worked both as a travelling salesman, and as a voluntary worker in a missionary

*A natural amphitheatre to hold cattle or pop, above the great loop
in the Boyne.*

hospital. Next he rattled around America for a spell – riding horses, 'doing a bit of this and that' – before going to Harvard, which sharpened his business acumen. And when he returned to London he embraced a sound commercial stint with the publishing house Faber & Faber. 'Then at 25, I was returned to Slane and found myself thrown in at the deep end.' Now, Henry is a member of a fistful of syndicates at Lloyds. His family owns property in Kent and the United States, in which he has strong interests. He is a complex and gifted character – articulate, energetic, a man with sharp imagination and the courage to put it to use. And quite plainly, he is amply gifted with a grasp of financial realities and understands the way in which money should be handled. However, he possesses two other characteristics that are of even greater importance to a responsible landowner. First and foremost he is an honest country-man. Secondly, and in all sincerity, he cares deeply for his inheritance.

He is insistent on the importance of rapidly putting Beau Parc's land back in good heart. 'Most of it,' he says, 'is let out on what we call 'conacre' – an Irish system meaning that it is leased on an eleven-month basis. Normally this runs from 1st January to 1st December. It's a system that can end up in being bad for the land. Too frequently you will find that neither tenant nor landlord is prepared to improve the holding, because neither of them feels ultimately responsible. The first thing I want to do is look at and improve the drainage and the fencing, make it secure for stock and run it properly.'

Many generations ago a Lady Fanny Conyngham married into the neighbouring Lambart family. This was at a time when the Lambarts were in financial difficulty. As rather a nice gesture, therefore, the second Marquess purchased Beau Parc from the Lambarts, to return it to them as a wedding present. 'Now,' says Henry, 'the last of the Lambarts has willed it back to me. And to be utterly truthful I only knew of the bequest on the morning I went to his funeral. I've known Beau Parc all my life, and I've loved its magical beauty. It's the sort of house anyone would be more than happy to live in. In a way the wheel has now turned full circle. You could say that Beau Parc has returned to the fold.'

Henry has fairly ambitious plans for that house. Slane Castle, too grand and imposing, is not at the peak of fashion today. Its aspect is austere, rooms too vast, and its scale out of touch with our times. Therefore, Henry Mount Charles and his second wife live in a flat upstairs, amid a comfortable jumble of modern art and decent old pieces off-set by the trappings of the electronics revolution that are part of the life of anyone in the world of business. The ground- and lower ground-floor rooms have been given over to commerce. With an alternative

Beau Park in the process of being restored to health.

Stand at Beau Parc, and everything in sight is Lord Mount Charles' domain.

'For me it's a source of strength and a bond': the castle and its unforgettable setting.

house on the estate, therefore, Henry feels that the sensible thing to do would be to concentrate the commercial side entirely on Slane and to control it from home a couple of miles away. The sensible option would be to live at Beau Parc.

When left to him, the fabric of Beau Parc was riddled throughout with dry-rot. This extended from roof timbers to cellars, walls to window frames. It was totally uninhabitable. Now Henry is in the process of doing it up. In the short term, while estate capital must still be bolstered, he plans to provide eight self-contained units which will accommodate rich American or Continental guests. 'We'll give them jacuzzis, telex, all mod cons.' And when the existing shooting system falls in – it has two years to run – he will be in a position to offer the finest accommodation for up to eight couples in the lap of luxury, and also to provide them with two days shooting. Then, in a few years time, Henry and his family will make Beau Parc their home. 'When I get old in the tooth, my wife and I will have a roof over our head while my son Alexander wrestles with the problems of Slane.'

Stand on the terrace above the Boyne at Beau Parc, and everything in sight is Lord Mount Charles' domain. He may have a way with money. He may be blessed with luck. He may be determined, outrageous, single-minded for success. But he also has a heart that beats in tune with the property. 'Fewer and fewer of these sort of places have survived in the south of Ireland. So many old estates in the Republic have come under the hammer, their timber flogged off, their land parcelled up for building. One gets the feeling of being one of the last of the Mohicans. But in a curious kind of way being the last of a breed makes you that much more bloody determined to make a go of it . . . determined not just for yourself but for the continuity of an estate, of the many other people dependant on the land, and of an ideal that reaches back into history. The decisions I make today affect not only me and my son who'll have to manage it in time. They also affect Gussie, who is a part of Slane, and Gus's family which is as rooted here as we are. . . .

'On Monday morning I fly to New York. That's just as about as divorced from this place as you could wish. But when I come back and come down the road from Dublin, I shall stop the car at the top of the bridge, and from there you see the whole place laid out in front of you. You look up the river and see the castle in the distance, and the trees, and the cattle on the riverside pasture, and the place gives you a very special feeling. For me it's a source of strength, and a bond. Although I do many other things in my life, I actually draw most of my inner strength from this place. And I know that just as this estate is part and parcel of me, it is part and parcel too, of all of who live and depend on Slane.'

Littlecote

Littlecote

Wiltshire:
Peter de Savary, Esquire

*H*ow does a man with a little money put by set about becoming established? In England the answer is short and simple: he buys a place in the country.

If owning a large country house is an indication of wealth, the ownership of land has always meant power. Since William I gave his principal followers land grants, in gratitude for their help and to consolidate the Conquest, and his barons, in turn, distributed manors among their lesser lords, those who have held land have held the reins of power. Until only a couple of generations ago this power was very real and it can still be apparent today.

In the old days, a landowner could count on his tenants to work his land, to fight for him, and to contribute to his wealth, either in money or in kind. The broader a man's acres, the greater his power. During the Middle Ages a landowner would have the support of everyone beneath him on the hierarchical pyramid. If he was a substantial lord, close to the Crown, his power would be displayed through the allegiance of dependent landowers. The household of a baron was maintained by gentlemen, or knights – the sons of his peers – who knew exactly where they slotted into the complex. The feudal system (the Latin *feodum* means 'fee') was structured on land tenure and the income from land, and on the fealty owing up the system and derived from those below.

A great lord would probably own several estates scattered across the shires, and he would maintain a stronghold on each of the principal ones. Until the 16th century these would certainly have been defensible. They might even have remained so until the 17th century when, after the Civil War, most castles on the instructions of Parliament, were 'slighted', or rendered militarily ineffective.

But if having your gatehouse and corner-towers blown up by

Cromwell put an end to your country home as a military power-base, it was to blossom with its land as a money-earner and remain firmly a symbol of your family's status. As such it would stand as power-collateral while you were wheeling and dealing at Court, perhaps, or in Westminster, or on the lucrative plains of India. When England's thrust made her a world power, the rich became almost a race apart. By then, as well as obtaining rents from their tenants, they could count on their votes as well; and a seat in Parliament led to further enrichment, and an even firmer hold on the land.

By the early 18th century, having accepted the necessity of education, the families in power found themselves hooked on 'culture'. Young men rumbled off in their carriages on the extensive Grand Tour of Europe, to come home with revolutionary, classical ideas absorbed so pleasurably under Italian skies. They returned with cartloads of paintings and statuary and similar up-market tourist trophies. They also returned with articulate opinions about the sort of houses they wanted to display them in. They commissioned porticoed mansions with symmetrical facades and stone steps zig-zagging to a raised front door. They sought to exemplify in the English countryside the principals of the architect Andrea Palladio who had flourished in Italy two centuries earlier. The Palladian influence, in

The ancillary buildings of a great country house can sometimes amount almost to a village in themselves. At Littlecote, these are presented with flair and enthusiasm and enable the ordinary visitor to bridge the centuries.

one form or another, was to dominate English country house design for generations to come.

This, then, was the use to which the new Englishman's castle was put: part art gallery, part declamation of cultivated taste. At the same time it continued to perform its now traditional roles of hunting lodge, pleasance, political powerhouse, guesthouse, home, and family flagship. The country house had become a man's retreat from London and, at the same time, his most prestigious shop window.

Young men on the make, like Longleat's John Thynne, knew well that to succeed in the power game they had to put their money into land and also have a house that proclaimed their position. These dynastic builders (as Mark Girouard has pointed out in his *Life in the English Country House*), were not necessarily farmers. Nor were their homes merely large houses in the country. While the land was both a symbol and a source of wealth, the house said a great deal more about its owner. It could say 'Look how rich I am!', or 'Look how cultivated!' And it could say 'Look at me and tremble, for I am the greatest man in the county.'

Not until the County Councils were established in 1886 did the landed aristocracy relinquish their hold on the shires. Meanwhile, the Industrial Revolution had created new tides of wealth. Those who acquired it were soon absorbed into the English system – as had been the successful merchants, the Tudor upstarts, the gentlemen of fortune and returned Nabobs from Bengal before them. Protective colouration was provided by their country houses and within a generation or two there remained but few differential cracks to cover.

Then, in the 19th century, a new breed was born. These were the millionaire tradesmen. They embraced brewers and bankers, mill-owners and munitions men; and they queued to join the ranks of the landed gentry. From the colonies, too, heavy with gold, sailed home the future 'Randlords' – hard, bronzed men with accents as broad as their shoulders – the Richard Hannays of this world who had beaten the hell out of some far-flung corner, or perhaps just hefted their pick for that final lucky strike. There even arrived the odd, self-exiled American, romantically viewing English country house life as the only life for a gent.

In England a ladder has always been at hand. Some of the new men built new country mansions. Others eased themselves into the homes of less adaptable families which had slithered down the snakes in the power game. Peter de Savary, a millionaire of the 'eighties, is every inch of this generation. But he is by no means new to the English scene. His stereotype has turned up in every century between the Conquest and Concorde. Tough, flexible, his eye on a whole stadium of goals, 'PDS' –

The Great Hall, Littlecote's noblest room. Here Peter de Savary dines when in residence to dream of the past – and future – of his house.

as he is known – has quarried a substantial fortune largely from oil and property. Yet he is one of a kind with the first John Thynne, and with the present Marquess of Bath, all three being gifted with a flair for success, all conspicuous for their panache. And like many successful men before him, PDS has acquired a grand country house. Littlecote, near Hungerford, at the Berkshire end of Wiltshire, has been continuously occupied since 1520 and probably replaces an even earlier house on the site. A long low sprawl of Elizabethan brick, peaked with gables, laced with flint-work, it sits like a grand, but now faded, dowager in the valley of the Kennet. Today, Littlecote is most certainly home to PDS. It is also, of course, both a symbol of his success, a financial investment, and his touchstone to history.

Traditionally, the property has comprised 4,500 acres of productive land as well as the house with its gardens, outbuildings, parkland and woods. This arrangement provided a balance for five and a half centuries. The land supported the house, the house ran the land. 'Now,' says PDS, 'the heart has been torn out of it' for in 1985 Peter de Savary bought the house from Sir David Seton Wills whose family had acquired Littlecote in 1922. He also acquired 100 acres – mainly parkland and amenity woods immediately round the house. Sir David continues to farm the bulk of the estate from a smaller house nearby. 'The only other kind of buyer,' says de Savary, 'would have been someone thinking in terms of a hotel . . . flats . . . weekend cottages. . . I could have made 25 units here – and sold them at a very nice profit. But commercialized like that, the character of Littlecote would have been destroyed for ever.'

Happily for Littlecote, PDS had set his mind on it being his private home. 'This is a beautiful house, alive and not in the least depressing. All right, so it has got 72 rooms. But it's compact in that there are only 12 bedroom suites. You can only put up a dozen couples. It is very liveable in and relaxed, and has a marvellous aura. It's both a privilege to live here and a pleasure.'

With no estate income, PDS recognized Littlecote's need for an annual support structure. He then laid the foundations for this with the determination of a man who gets things done by yesterday.

There was a lot for the public to enjoy, even before he started: the fine mosaics of the 'Orphic Hall', part of an extensive Romano-British villa in the park and, of course the house itself. Rooms range from the country's sole surviving Cromwellian chapel – bare of ornament, in the strict

Covered and forgotten until re-excavation in 1900, the mosaics of the Romano-British 'Orphic Hall' are among the finest in Britain.

'Every inch of this generation': Peter de Savary outside his Wiltshire home.

Puritan code – with its railed gallery and stark box-pews, to the celebrated 'Dutch Parlour' whose walls and ceiling, even the door, were, in the early 18th century, given their *trompe l'oeil* decoration and the illusion of being densely hung with pictures. PDS bought Littlecote lock, stock and barrel. In doing so, he was to acquire one of England's greatest collective treasures: two-thirds of the entire surviving stock of Civil War armour. The uniforms, to this day remarkably pristine, comprise coats made from ox-hide with the texture of suede and colour of dark buff yellow. Together with the associated pistols, carbines, muskets and edged weapons, the breastplates, helmets and accoutrements both cavalry and infantry, they were crucial to the presentation of the Civil War theme PDS planned as the focal public attraction. The armour alone cost him a cool half million pounds.

'Obviously, the Royal Armouries were keen to acquire it. But then I was offered a million by an American collector. So I put it to the Tower that they could become owners of this historic collection for only half its market value. I even chipped in with 20 grand as a kick off for their purchasing fund.' The bait was taken, and de Savary further ensured that the collection stays on permanent loan at Littlecote, where it has lain since it was last used in the mid-17th century.

Such manipulation of resources is typical. You can see it as he balances

Two-thirds of England's total stock of Cromwellian armour is secure within the walls of Littlecote: buff coats of oxhide, cavalry carbines, and the breastplates and helmets of Colonel Popham's men.

The genius of Lyn Kramer, today's Madame Tussaud, provided PDS with his waxwork figures which roll back the years to the summer of 1642.

*A major public attraction is the tilt yard. Genuine blows are exchanged
in the jousting.*

deals on the telephone. Having negotiated a million pounds' worth of armour for a mere £20,000, PDS turned to the house where he foresaw a safe flood of visitor revenue. One third of the house was immediately rewired. 'Nine and a half miles of wire, would you believe?' A public route was planned through a series of downstairs rooms where an episode was recreated from Littlecote's past – the summer of 1642. Tableaux were commissioned and set up incorporating waxworks, Littlecote's militaria, and an audio background with special lighting effects.

Meanwhile, a Herculean labour was got under way outside. Four bulldozers were set loose to clear out the jungle before grass was re-seeded. A rose garden was planted where before there had been a car park, five knot gardens in place of a lawn, four herb gardens, a herbaceous border, and a medicinal garden. If PDS had the ideas – frequently revised – the man engaged to put them into practise was George Stretfield – former Kenya farmer and soldier who had 'retired' as a project manager. George was brought in as Littlecote's estate manager. His tasks included reconstructing a 17th-century village . . . setting up a rare breeds farm with its necessary buildings . . . providing an adventure playground here and a stockaded 'fort' there . . . ensuring the proper interpretation of the Roman villa and its archaeological significance . . . building the shops, licensed restaurant, refreshment kiosks, lavatories, and seeing to the car parking and ticketing . . . providing for falconry displays and mewses to house working birds of prey. . . . 'I even became a railway engineer,' he recalls, as a miniature train wheezed consumptively up the straight beyond an ornamental arm of the Kennet. 'And we had to move this water. And plant 4,000 roses – in March '86! Remember the state of the ground at the time?' George Stretfield smiles readily when asked how long it all took. 'I started work on 2 December 1985. We were ready for opening exactly 90 days later.'

Under George Stretfield and farm manager Howard Paton, there is a summer staff of 115, reducing in winter to 46. When PDS took over there were only four. He opens Littlecote as a summer attraction. 'In the winter it's purely private and represents the quality side of life.' The farming operation revolves around the rare breeds station. At the end of the summer they sell off stock to cut labour and the cost of fodder, buying-in again in the spring, when the grazing has returned. 'Only a very small number is maintained off-season, and then only if this is worth the candle from a breeding point of view.'

Birds of prey from falcons to buzzards, and this dignified snowy owl,
are loosed to the delight of spectators.

A lanner falcon attacks the lure.

*Rare breeds include poultry which could have strutted straight from
a Chinese lacquer screen.*

One of the Labours of Hercules undertaken by ex-soldier George Stretfield was to construct an Alamo-type fort for modern-day skirmishes.

Captivated – lock, stocks and barrel!

During your first year in this business, if you've any marketing skills, you can expect to pull in the crowds. But the summer of 1986 limped in, long overdue, across fields iron-hard for months; and the Americans failed to arrive at all: they remained locked up at home with their self-imposed fears over Libya. Yet despite these drawbacks, PDS is gratified that his visitors numbered a creditable 118,000. 'Our annual operating costs, indoors and out, run to £900,000. And that's before looking for catastrophe maintenance – major repairs to the roof, say, or eradicating rising damp. So we have to aim at 300,000 visitors a year by 1988. The 1987 target is 200,000.'

And, having attained this goal with its heavy influx and inevitably some loss of privacy, will PDS still continue his love affair with Littlecote? 'Oh yes, indeed I will . . . because this is my home you see.'

Ask then how long it would take to dismantle the fittings – to clear Littlecote of its waxworks, gazebos, tea-houses and so on, to disperse the rare breeds, pack up the jousting, pay off the staff and remove the miniature railway. 'How long?' repeats PDS, eyes snapping at the challenge. 'Give me two days indoors, a month at the most outside.' Next, as if caught out, he grins at you broadly, and then for a moment appears to relax while contemplating the tip of an unlit Havanna. A moment later, however, he'll look you in the eye. 'But I won't do it,' he'll say. 'Or if I do – put it this way – if I do I shall not be leaving the house. Because I've bought Littlecote as my country home in England, and I can tell you that I'm planning for it to remain my home.'

Achnacarry

Achnacarry

Inverness-shire:
Sir Donald Cameron of Lochiel

'*I* don't think I could be happy anywhere else.'

Sir Donald Cameron of Lochiel is standing in front of his four-square and compact little Scottish castle set in the best part of 100,000 of the most spectacular acres in Britain.

Couched on flat land furnished with paddocks and trees and neatly tended gardens, Achnacarry's policies – its immediate grounds – are welcoming and tranquil. Its wider setting, however, displays a rapid transition from the half-tamed to the wild. This is a countryside rich in magnificent contrasts: tumbling water from the streaming hills; vast lochs reflecting the changing skies; on two sides, seemingly topless mountains providing stepping stones for the gods, while closer to hand there is a dramatic crag – a plug of granite hung with larch and clanged by wheeling crows. As the hoodie flies, Lochiel's home rests nine miles north-east of the castle at Fort William, while in both geographical and spiritual respects it resides at the heart of the Cameron country. It is Lochiel's pride that, by unbroken descent from father to son for 16 generations, he is the hereditary Chief of the Clan Cameron.

'Originally,' he explains, 'the chief lived on an island in Loch Eil, one of the three major lochs on the estate. Next he built a place called Tor Castle on the banks of the river Lochy, about five miles from Fort William on the site of an old castle. And then of course in about 1660, or somewhere around that time, Fort William was built by the English as one of the forts to keep the Highlands in order. It was garrisonned by English troops, and Sir Ewen Cameron, my ancestor, thought the fort a bit too close to be healthy, so he moved out here and built a house – not this one – in the

Water tumbling from Loch Arkaig.

1660s. Very little is known about that house except from a report I have, written in 1772, which refers to the old house as being a wooden building with stone gables. It was burned down in 1746 after the 'Forty-Five; but there is still a stone gable outside by the main gate which is a part of that original house. Then the estate was forfeited – confiscated by the Crown – because my ancestor had thrown in his lot with Prince Charlie . . . and we didn't get it back until about 1784 when we had to pay a large fine to the government of the day.   .

'My great-great-grandfather, whose portrait you can see by Raeburn – he was only a young boy at the time – he got it back and started building this present house in 1805. He was largely brought up in France and didn't quite appreciate it here. In fact he never finished building Achnacarry which was left to his son, my great-grandfather, to complete in about 1830. We have lived here ever since. The only break was during the War when it was occupied by Commandos. Indeed, it became the Commando base. They did a certain amount of damage to the house and had a bad fire that burned the whole of the hall and roof. So when we got it back after the War there was a lot to do to restore it. This was really a blessing in disguise. The house needed to be reorganized for modern use anyway. We closed down the basement altogether, to bring the kitchen up, with new back stairs and much else besides. But as I say, there was a lot to do, and it was very difficult because there was a shortage of materials, and in those days everything was rationed. Nevertheless, we eventually got it restored, and by about 1950 or 1951 it was more or less ready for habitation.'

Lochiel was commissioned in the Lovat Scouts as a Territorial, when he was at Oxford University, and became their Colonel in Italy towards the end of the war. Today he must certainly be among the most youthful-looking of men within a caber's toss of 80. Lochiel was Honorary Colonel of the 4th/5th Cameron Highlanders, has represented the Queen as Lord Lieutenant for Inverness-shire, and has been honoured by her as a Knight of the Thistle, the country's highest order of chivalry after the Order of the Garter and the premier honour in Scotland. Yet of all his duties and privileges, Lochiel regards those of being the Camerons' hereditory Clan Chief as among the most important in his life.

'We are planning a Clan museum down the road there, in the old post office in the village – a lovely old listed building which we're in the process of restoring. As you can imagine, it will attract clansfolk and others from all parts of the United Kingdom, as well as visitors from places like New Zealand and the United States researching their Cameron forebears.' Only last year he and Lady Cameron returned from a round-the-world

Sir Donald Cameron of Lochiel, 16th hereditary Chief of the Clan Cameron.

tour organized by Cameron associations. It is a modest cause for satisfaction to Lochiel that Canada and the United States alone boast a dozen branches of the Clan association, each numbering perhaps 150 families. 'Certainly we were introduced to 2,000 member of the Clan in Australia, and quite as many in New Zealand. These tours make for a wonderful feeling of solidarity and family unity.'

As well as on the occasions of these periodical goodwill tours, Camerons are able to get together at the Clan gatherings held every five years in August. These take place at Achnacarry, the focal point for Camerons wherever they may live. The next gathering is due in 1989, when anything from 800 to 1,000 Camerons may be expected to turn up, including 200 or more from overseas. Cameron Clan gatherings are not much different from other family reunions, in that they are occasions for friendships to be renewed and new ties cemented. But at Achnacarry they are conducted on a larger and a grander scale. They also, by tradition, have an accent on country activities particularly relevant to the Highlands. 'There's a big marquee for tea and smaller ones for sales and Clan displays. We have the local pipe band . . . Highland dancing . . . the tug-of-war – a great excitement, that – between the estate and the Clan. . . . Then there's six-a-side shinty, clay pigeon shooting, sheep dog demonstrations, and the march past with pipes and banners and all the rest of it. I must confess that it's the greatest of fun. There are, I am afraid, rather a lot of speeches, but it goes without saying that I am delighted to make the house open to everybody. In 1938,' Lochiel recalls somewhat wistfully, 'my father started a visitors book for all those involved to write their names in. I've tried to keep this up. Last time, though, we had a bit of a drama. At the eleventh hour,' he confesses, 'the book suddenly vanished. Eventually it was run to earth with my dog – most disloyally – attempting to devour it. It was a close-run thing . . . but the records were saved.'

The northern part of Scotland is separated from the southern by Glen Mor, the Great Glen as it is commonly known. This geological fault cleaves the map as clean as a claymore, gashing north-east from the Irish to the North Seas. Navigable throughout its length, it comprises a string of long narrow lochs from Loch Linnhe in the west to Loch Ness in the east, where at Inverness it flows as the river Ness into the Moray Firth and the sea. Nowhere is its surface appreciably above sea level. The town of Fort William is sited in the Glen, while Achnacarry itself stands on flat low ground abut 150 feet above its waters.

The mountains that form much of Cameron of Lochiel's estate thus appear even higher and more dramatic than if viewed from upland terrain. His land, moreover, extends to within sight of Britain's highest

Gairlochy, the hamlet hard by Achnacarry.

mountain, Ben Nevis, known in these parts from love and familiarity simply as 'The Ben'. This is a hard land of granite and shallow acid soils – raw, unyielding country where to compete you must be as tough as the environment you live in. Much of it lies over the 1,000-foot contour. The walking is rough, the winds keen, and the winters of a quality to daunt the average Sassenach, cosseted in the gentle Saxon south. Great arms of water thrust between the mountains – sea-lochs, salty from the open seas, and fresh-water lochs imprisoned by the hills that feed them. Rightly, it is due to the hardy Celts that through fitness and inheritance the Highlands have been secured.

'As 16th Clan Chief, and because my family has been involved so long with these parts, I should find it quite impossible to live anywhere else. There are many reasons for this. My love for this place is of the deepest nature. To live in the ancestral heart of your clan country is – to me – something rare and unique. I am sure that my son feels the same way as I do, and that his son, in turn, will share this feeling for this country and with the people associated with it. The estate, in fact, belongs to my son to

Loch Lochy seen from Gairlochy. Glen Roy holds the background.

whom I made it over some years ago, and I manage it for him and in collaboration with him.'

Life in these parts is by no means easy. It might be supposed, from watching the shepherds gathering the sheep as they come pouring off the hill, that there's money to be made from sheep husbandry. 'In theory,' laments Lochiel, 'I suppose there might be – if only one could get a decent lambing percentage.' A man with 100 ewes does very well when he achieves 90 per cent, or even 80 per cent of surviving lambs to ewes, and can feel lucky to get as much as 60 per cent. In parts of England, by contrast, where ewes habitually give birth to two or more lambs, the percentage can be very much higher. 'But we are pushing up the percentage all the time. One reason for this is that when we've got them off the hill we put the ewes into parks, into our low-lying deer parks protected by fencing. On the hill, of course, the sheep get illnesses, they drown, they get killed by foxes, and when you count them after they're gathered you'll invariably find fewer than you had hoped for or expected.'

Despite these problems, however, agriculture is one of the four main legs that support the estate. Lochiel ticks these off on the fingers of a hand as farming, forestry, tourism, sport, and then pauses to gather his thoughts.

'Even in the 'twenties and 'thirties, life was very difficult for my father. Sheep were unprofitable in those days, and the one way he could keep the place going was by advantageous sporting lets. Diversification, as it might be called, was in this way already an accepted practice well before the War. Today it must be developed on an even larger scale if the land and its community are to remain healthy.' Indeed, Lochiel recalls how, as a young man, he started business-life as a chartered accountant, working for Imperial Tobacco in London. Since the estate was unable to support him, he had, to a certain degree, to go and earn his own living.

The farming interests at Achnacarry are centred around 6,000 ewes – mainly Black-faced Sheep – and 150 commercial beef cattle. The latter principally comprise 120 cross-bred cows that produce, on average, 115 calves a year in spring and autumn. Each year, 15 calves are bought in and there will always be about 50 young breeding stock coming on.

The stockman is Malcolm Cameron, now in his early thirties. 'I came to the job for a short while,' he laughs quietly, 'and have stayed for 17 years.' Cattle are his passion. He cares for them as if they were his own family. This must be one reason why he has remained at Achnacarry. Another is that he is given a free hand in the management of the cattle. Naturally, however, Malcolm will go and confer with Lochiel about important matters such as buying stock and what the estate should expect at the sales.

One of Malcolm Cameron's own special family.

Calves are sold on either at six months, in the auction market nearby which the estate has an interest in, or else at about nine months old in Stirling. These forward stores are chiefly crosses. The bright new stars at Achnacarry are the two recently introduced Limousin bulls whose progeny are proving most effective. Crosses are also produced from their longer-established Charolais bull, and there are some splendid-looking Highland crosses to be seen grazing below the upper road to Fort William. Malcolm is a man truly dedicated to his work, always seeking new ways to improve his stock. In his job there's no guarantee of knocking off at sundown, or of packing it in for a month in the summer. And Malcolm works alone, except that in winter one shepherd and an estate gamekeeper will help him feed the young stock. The cattle are kept out all year round, and, like the men who tend them, are extremely hardy.

'To be honest, though,' Lochiel is forced to admit, 'cattle on a Highland estate is not a profitable business. You've got to buy in most of your feed, which is very expensive at £150 or £175 per cow, and £400 or thereabouts means a good price for your calves. So when you add on wages, transport and everything else, the margin just isn't there. It may be for reasons of sentiment perhaps, but I know I should be very chary of giving up the cattle. However, a lot of people up here have moved out of commercial beef cattle, and one can't really blame them.'

With little more than 100 acres under grass or oats capable of making into silage, only a quarter of the total feed is estate produced. 'Until recently,' Lochiel explains, 'we'd feed the cattle draff from the local distillery. That was rather a good thing, and splendid for the beasts, although no-one could pretend it was cheap. But then they gave up making whiskey.' Currently, the estate is buying feed in compressed form, as nuts. It's a case of keeping a weather eye out for whatever may be available for an economic price.

Yet if the larger landowners are moving out of beef production, there are still crofters and other smallholders – including Malcolm's winter-helping shepherd – who put their own stock in at the local auction-cum-show. Everyone turns up to these affairs. Most of the shepherds come to run an appraising eye over their neighbours as much as the beasts, because these are social as well as working occasions when gossip is exchanged. If he can fit it in, Lochiel normally likes to attend and he'll be seen mingling with the people from his estate, confering with Malcolm Cameron, checking prices. If luck smiles on him, Malcolm may walk away with a prize or two; and if not, it has still been an occasion of excitement and interest to all whose lives revolve around animals.

'But it's sheep,' maintains Lochiel, 'that are the main thing here. Yet I am afraid even sheep depend a lot on the subsidies. In fact, I regard the subsidies we receive as providing primarily a social benefit. The advancement of agriculture is really only secondary.' Lochiel's argument runs that, from a purely economic standpoint, sheep subsidies cannot be sound agricultural policy. 'In objective terms, sheep are probably not sensible here. But if we believe, as I do very firmly, in the importance of keeping the people on the ground in the Highlands, then you've got to give them some sort of help towards farming or else they'd just pack up, sell off, and the land would become barren. And if you believe this, then obviously the sensible solution is to provide a subsidy for sheep.'

Any encouragement of this kind is to be welcome on the estate. Lochiel's property supports not only his own 6,000 sheep but also all those owned by the crofters. About 100 crofters maintain small holdings on land embraced by the estate, putting their own sheep out on common grazing not touched by the estate sheep. And there is an additional and very telling argument in favour of encouraging sheep farming on Achnacarry. Without the input of the shepherds on the hills, and the essential roles in the community life that are played by their families, the estate would be unable to sustain an efficient operation in its other activities.

Stockman Malcolm Cameron collects yet another prize.

Like the cattle, sheep are bred here mainly for meat, only about 10 per cent or so of the revenue being for wool. They are gathered in June from the high ground and the lambs sold on as stores. Lambs are fattened for sale in the parks. A recent development, which the estate is confident will pay dividends, has been the purchase of 350 acres of good lowland arable where ewes can be sent for over-wintering. This is down by Clackmannan, east of Stirling, in an area enjoying a kinder climate than the Highlands. It recalls the practise followed in the last century when ewes were driven off for wintering in the comparative mildness of the lowlands.

In late September, sheep are brought down to be dipped, and it can be a magical sight to watch them being gathered. Miles away you see the mountain where they will be coming from, perhaps brilliant green in the sun. You wait and watch until you gradually become aware of a sprinkling of tiny white dots like grains of sand on the top. Slowly, and seemingly at random, the dots move down the face of the hill, and as they flow and separate and merge again they can be seen no longer as trailing sand: it is as if an endless necklace has suddenly broken and pearls are cascading down the mountain. It may be over an hour from your first sighting before the sheep reach the spot where you are stationed, and by then it has become apparent that their course – far from random – has, all along, been eased, checked, modified and controlled by the fine dogs which are in turn directed by the shepherds.

Half a dozen shepherds will have been involved. There's Donnie McPherson, Lochiel's head shepherd, and John Redpath with the distinction of having tasted the wider world out there. John's venture to the south ended with a job with Sainsbury's in London; and it was doubtless the stresses of that hard urban existence that made him foreswear alcohol and head home to the hill.

When the sheep are down, they are plunged through the dip, and there comes the serious business of counting. And if this is God's own country, the time now comes when its one flaw hits you – literally – in the face: midges descend in a cloud on the gathering to persecute everyone, Sassenach or Scot. Even the shepherds say they never get used to them.

A glance at the Ordnance map shows that timber in this region grows to the 900 foot contour and no higher – the cut-off level for growth. The open moors and mountains emerge like islands from a green sea.

'Forestry,' explains Lochiel, 'our second commercial leg, is concentrated on the sort of trees which do best in our local conditions. These are predominantly larch, Sitka and Norway spruce. I suppose,' he recalls 'that we've planted up about 1,000 new acres ourselves.' By and large,

'Pearls cascading down the mountain . . . reach the spot where you are stationed. . .'

Master of the situation.

Their course has been far from random.

however, the estate follows its long-term programme of planting, thinning, felling and extraction which is balanced and requires little innovation.

Thinnings are taken out at 15 to 20 years, and at 40 or 50 the timber is clear felled. 'We space it out so that there's always some wood coming along, and we are able to do this firstly because we are fortunate enough to have the acreage, and secondly because our forestry is well established.'

As with all activities on this estate, forestry recognizes the demands of other disciplines such as farming and sport, and it also recognizes the character of the countryside. This is exemplified in the way the timber has been spread across the landscape.

It is an estate policy that trees are disposed in blocks which neither blanket the landscape nor extend to more than about 1,000 acres. Because the trees only grow to 900 feet, unity is retained in the landscape where it rises above that line. Ample space is also left between the blocks to give access down from the hill, for the movements of deer and sheep are in response to seasonal factors of weather and the availability of grazing. 'The trouble then is that you've got to deer fence your trees to keep the deer out of the plantations. And that's very expensive, despite the grants.' Labour, too, is flexible: it is a noticeably happy and natural feature of this estate that if a forestry job is to be done and there are shepherds at hand, then the latter will readily pitch in to help, just as estate workers of all persuasions will help when it comes to rounding up sheep.

Compared to selling lambs, the production of timber is very much a long-term business. Until recently, however, Lochiel used to have a return almost on his doorstep. Felled logs would be delivered to the pulp mill that had been established down the road at Fort William. Unhappily, that outlet has now closed its doors, so new markets – one has recently emerged at Stirling – have to be sought out. There is also considerable cooperation between the estate and the Forestry Commission to which Lochiel has sold about 15,000 acres of woodland under the 'feu' system (not unlike a long lease) and then taken back the sporting rights. Nor is all the timber confined to commercial soft-woods. Lochiel's grandfather planted a large number of oak trees which remain a feature of the more sheltered ground, while beeches also do particularly well.

The principal factors in what Lochiel calls tourism are the cottages he lets and a more substantial house which is let from May until his son moves in in August. Clunes, the dower house where Lochiel's father was living when he died, has been done up with great care to make an

The serious business of counting – made no easier by the midges!

Timber grows to the 900ft contour – and no higher.

RIGHT:*'Forestry is our second commercial leg.'*

extremely comfortable let. Here again, the estate demonstrates its close-knit approach to the deployment of available talent. The management of the estate's accommodation for letting is handled by Lady Cameron, the wife of Lochiel, while the housekeeping is the concern of a stalker's wife.

'We've got two little cottages down on Loch Lochy, and a very nice one on Loch Arkaig which we like to let to fishermen. And because there's good fishing on that loch we also let out boats – by the day or the week – and these are looked after by an estate joiner who also collects the money.'

Loch Arkaig is a freshwater loch about 14 miles long. 'It's a big loch and therefore can't really be stocked so to all intents and purposes has to look after itself.' Loch Arkaig has for two years now also been the scene of a fish farming venture that was launched in 1985 by a firm called Marine Harvest, a subsidiary of Unilever. 'This is quite a bonus for the estate. What they do is get the salmon straight from the hatcheries and put them on our loch in cages. They feed them and keep them here for about nine months until they are ready to enter the salt water.' When that stage arrives the fish are about one year old, and the company transfers them in tanks to another set of cages anchored in a sea-loch where they continue to put on weight until they are sold. As an interesting contrast to this highly technical operation, the estate is host on Loch Lochy to a very much smaller enterprise which is currently farming rainbow trout. This business is more in the nature of a one-man venture, and the estate leases both the water and a house.

Lochiel's final commercial leg is sport. 'There are no grouse here now to speak of, although pre-war the house would be let for the season. In those days they used to shoot over dogs, and our tenants could look forward to, I suppose, about a hundred brace.' Although Achnacarry is now no longer grouse country, there's still a fair chance of coming across the odd pheasant in the woods and policies around the house. 'But these pheasants,' Lochiel claims with a chuckle, 'they're no more than a luxury, just kept for fun. . . . No, the great thing up here – and very good it is, too – is the deer stalking.'

Above the tree-line, the high moorland that covers 90 per cent of the estate is the home of large numbers of red deer. Each year the deer population has to be culled, to control their numbers and thus ultimately to maintain the vegetation they subsist on, thereby maintaining their quality. And because such a degree of skill and excitement is involved in approaching and despatching a stag, this estate – like other great Highland properties – offers commercial stag shooting in the late summer, either by the week or fortnight.

Most stalking clients tend to be from the Continent – notably from

Loch Arkaig.

Marine Harvest's salmon cages anchored on the loch.

A well-earned breather on a long, hard stalk.

Germany, Belgium, Denmark and Sweden, and probably in that order. A number of sportsmen, however, come year after year to Achnacarry from other countries, and there are still those in the United Kingdom who are drawn here for the stalking. The economics of deer stalking are vital to the community. Not only do the stalkers pay a £125 fee for each stag they shoot, but the estate itself keeps the venison which it then sells through the meat trade at the current market price. Last year this fluctuated between 60p and 90p a pound. The price varies considerably because it is dominated by the German market, and it is never easy to budget ahead. But a twelve stone stag – that's twelve stone of meat after the removal of guts, head, feet and hide – is likely to fetch about the same again as the fee the client has paid for shooting it. In terms of game fees and the sale of venison alone, therefore, a single beast could be worth £250 to the estate; and since some 150 stags are killed each year, their gross yield may be reckonned as somewhere around the £36,000 mark. 'Against this,' Lochiel is quick to add, 'has to be set all the expenditure – wages for stalkers and gillies, transport costs which are very heavy, winter feeding of stags, and management charges. So there is not much left over in the end.'

For those uninitiated in the language of the hill, a confusion can arise from the use of the word 'stalker'. On the one hand it denotes the client, the punter paying out good money for his sport. On the other, it also describes the experienced and knowledgeable employee of the estate. It is the latter's job to watch over the deer and, during the stag shooting season which normally lasts for about seven weeks from the middle of August, to take charge of the client and organize his sport. At other times of the year, apart from in the winter months when the hinds are killed, he will turn a hand elsewhere on any of the varied tasks that this multi-disciplined property demands, such as vermin control – killing foxes – or fencing perhaps, or forestry work, or helping the shepherds.

The estate currently employs three stalkers. The head stalker, a young man called Alec McDonald, only recently took over the position from his father, while for Alistair Morrice, whom you would place in his late thirties, 1986 was his first season as a fully-fledged stalker. Alistair used to be a handyman round the estate. Having, however, worked the hill for years as a gillie, he has an enviable accumulation of skill and knowledge. There isn't any real heirarchy: they work as a team and are closely bonded. And they are also a privileged breed. It goes without saying that a stalker is extremely tough physically. In addition, they each possess an intimate knowledge of the terrain, know the ways of the red deer, know indeed each individual beast in order to select the particular beasts to be killed. In just the same way as Lochiel gives Malcolm Cameron a pretty free hand with the cattle, so it is with his stalkers. Once a year the stalkers meet to determine the number of beasts to be shot in each forest. The decision is theirs. The men are responsible and dedicated, and this is reflected in the respect in which they are held.

On the hill the stalker is king. He is of the stuff to take complete command of the situation and the client. A first-class stalker can be a hard task master. Before an unknown sportsman – say a Düsseldorf business-man – may even put his boot on the hill, he will be obliged to prove his marksmanship to the satisfaction of the stalkers . . . and if the client fails on the rifle range to show he's up to scratch, there will be no chance of his aligning his sights on a beast. The last thing any professional or sportsman needs is the company of a dangerous cowboy's, or someone else's, wounded beast which he will have to follow up and despatch himself. Once on the hill, too, after a punishing stint that may take several hours to approach where the deer are gathered, it is an unbroken rule that the client unquestionably obeys the stalker to the letter. 'Git doon, mon.' 'Stop talking there.' 'Get a move on.' 'Lie still.' 'Take the beast on the left – the ten-pointer with the damaged right foreleg.'

Achnacarry has three deer forests spread across its 100 square miles of barren moorland. These are called the North Forest, the South Forest, and Achdalieu, and each provides roughly 50 stags a year. Each forest, too, is the responsibility of its individual stalker.

From November to January, when the deer leave the snows of the high ground for shelter and feed in the woodland, the hinds are culled by the stalkers and their assistants. These last are the gillies. Anyone can come along and be a gillie – it's a casual job, for a limited period – but they have to be strong and supremely fit. They may be young shepherds, or the sons of Lochiel's shepherds, or even a young sportsman who welcomes a hard time on the hill and will grasp at the chance to learn more about his craft; and most of them aspire to becoming a stalker one day. The gillies are the Sherpas of the hill – part porter, part runner, part Argocat driver, part dogsbody. But these mid-winter months see them out in the silent woods with the estate's four full-time stalkers. This is a time when they hone their skills and sharpen their knowledge of the ways of deer as they select and weed out the hinds, leaving the optimum number to maintain a healthy stock in each forest, and so that the land is not over-stocked

In the same way, in late summer, when stags are the quarry of the stalker, it is the gilly who does the heavy work – that is, unless the stalking client has the experience for such tasks himself. When a stag is shot, the gilly removes the gralloch (or stomach), disembowelling the beast there

and then on the hillside, to leave the innards for the crows and foxes. The party will already have walked steadily up-hill for hours, through knee-high heather and across peat bogs that suck at each step. No one has been able to stop for a breather. Once the stalker's telescope has picked out the deer, the party will have taken a line hidden from the beasts with no deviations and no slackening of pace. The weather, too, is never fully predictable. One moment it has you sweating like a pig, the next boring through hail which it decides to sling at you horizontally. So, when the client has killed his stag and can relax for a while over his smoke, it is the gillie's job to get the carcase off the hill – or at best help the client to bring it down. This is by no means as easy as it may sound. The gillie, like the stalker and client, might well be soaked to the skin as well as feeling clobbered from the going. It could be the case that the client is not as fit as could be desired and that he is reacting petulantly in consequence. But, whatever, the gillie is the one to remain unshakeable throughout. He will be calm, helpful, ever available, and willing to heft or heave the carcase down to the point where the 'Argo', an all-terrain vehicle, can take it on board for the game larder.

Stalking clients are put up on the estate, and of course they all want to rent Clunes. The dower house lies only a mile or so from Achnacarry, and it gives them that little touch of luxury. A comfortable night in civilized surroundings is an essential antedote to strenuous action. After a heavy day on the hill, the client may justifiably decide against making a heavy night of it, too. But at the end of his week-long or two weeks' assault course, after pushing himself across country and shivering in peat bog, the now hardened, wind-burned and slimmed-down client sometimes makes the 15-minute car journey to the Spean Bridge Hotel. Here, on the final Saturday night, the departing client might bump into the incoming party, and tales of Marathon marches and superhuman stalks will be exchanged in the most amazing brands of English. Meanwhile, when the door opens, great gusts of revelry come surging in from the other bar, for the stalkers and gillies have been handed their tips, and alcohol is being eased down relaxing throats. Soon, one by one, these will approach the clients, and over a dram or three of single malt they and the Belgians (or the Dutch or the Germans) will relive the triumphs and wash away the disasters that have created bonds between them. Now it is that the Highlanders gently tease the departing sportsmen, and tell them perhaps – but only in truth – how well they performed while pitting themselves against the elements

The kill. Stalker Alistair Morrice (left) with his client from Sweden.

103

Down off the hill, the now hardened client can relax in idyllic country.

and the terrain and the wary stags – in pitting themselves, as they say, against the hill.

'I shoot deer in Scotland,' you may hear a client say, 'because Scotland provides the best sport in the world. Here the stag and the sportsman have an equal chance, and you need the cunning and stamina of a stag yourself if you are to shoot him.' 'Last month, in my country,' claims another, 'I shot twenty deers in one hour. I was in the tree and they came close underneath for the food. This week, I shot a single stag, and I feel more proud of that one than of all the others.'

Now, over their whiskeys, the stalkers will talk about their life on the estate, and you learn how this great enterprise keeps going on a basic staff of ten shepherds, four maintenance men, three stalkers and a stockman, with the professional input of the land agents firm West Highland Estate Office and of Jock Hunter who acts as factor to Lochiel. You learn, too, about the poachers who get more deer than the estate, and of how they have just slaughtered more than a dozen hinds, stags and whatever they got their sights on in the blinding glare of their headlamp beams. They go on to relate how the meat is sold to less than scrupulous butchers; and they'll murmur also, with a deeper kind of bitterness, about wounded deer now limping on the hill, and of the poachers' neglect of the clean kill.

And eventually they come round to the man at the focus of the estate, on whose decisions hang the future of the wide community. 'Lochiel,' they say, 'a very fair man. Aye, he's a good man to have at Achnacarry.' To one side, meanwhile, a pair of hardened stalkers will be wrestling with the pronunciation of a Belgian factory-owner, while on the other a shepherd with the mildness of his calling explains how he tried to give up the drink, and on a third a budding young army officer, filling in as gilly before the Coldstream Guards and displaying more than a touch of the John MacNabs, tells how having just covered 23 punishing miles he has been tipped a mere £5 for his week-long pains. . . . But while the decibels soar and the spirits are sunk, one common link serves to bind together both shepherd and stalker, gilly and woodman, barmaid, Ben-climber or Belgian businessman – a bond which up here, in Britain's ultimate wilderness, goes by the simple name: 'the hill'.

Ebberston Hall

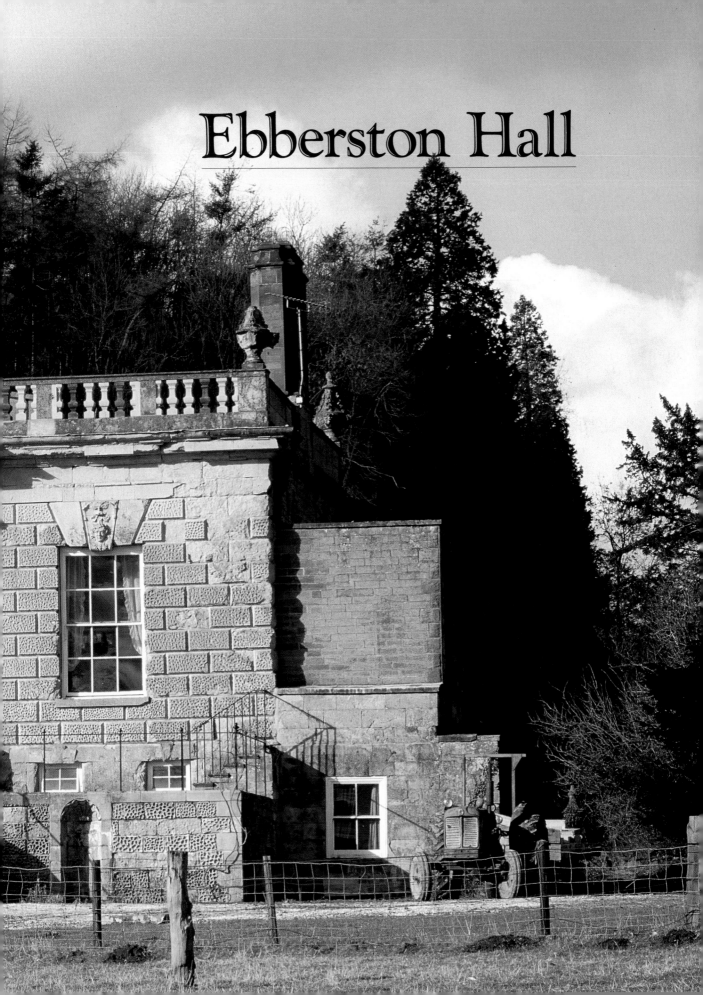

Ebberston Hall

North Yorkshire:
West de Wend Fenton, Esquire

Some are born to land, some achieve it, and some have landowning thrust upon them. Even before its adaptation, this quotation sounds with a crackpot ring. Reverse its sentiments, however, and it comments on the misfortunes of those under whom land diminishes – the losers, one might say, to their predecessors' management, to their own inadequacies, or to third-party influences beyond their control. Clearly there are many other admirable and valid reasons for why a man's landed property can become smaller. It is not uncommon, for a start, for a landowner to sell up and switch into other ventures. Nor is it unknown for a family quite genuinely to feel it socially wrong to be in possession of large and valuable estates these days while the not so fortunate have to settle for less. Such families have transferred vast acreages into the ownership of the National Trust, because the Trust opens doors for ordinary people to places – and reactions – that were in former years confined largely to the privileged. For yet another category it is a matter, on weighing priorities, of concluding that circumstances oblige them to release land in the interests of more important factors.

Among the latter must be numbered West de Wend Fenton. Born to an old and large agricultural estate on the other side of Yorkshire, West now finds himself farming little more than 50 acres. Against this, however – and against all the odds – he and his wife Margaret have successfully rescued one of the most important, and certainly the smallest, Palladian house in the kingdom. This is Ebberston Hall, a delectable jewel of a countryman's home with its back to the gritty and grouse-rich moors and its face lifted to the smiling Vale of Pickering.

If the first exponent of Palladian architecture in England had been that 17th-century Jack-of-all-trades and master of each with the unforgettable name of Inigo Jones, it was left to the Grand Tour that became the rage 100 years later to boost Palladianism into the British charts and make it the number-one hit in the shires. During his 19 months in Italy from 1613, young Inigo Jones, still in his thirties, made a dual study of the ruins of classical Rome and the buildings around Venice that had been designed a century before by Andrea Palladio. At the same time, he devoured Palladio's published works both on the ancient buildings of Rome and on the architectural theories he had developed. The English architect was as captivated by the Italian's theoretical observations as by their application in practice. In essence, Palladio (whose major buildings date from 1549) had worked up and evolved the long-established theories of 'harmonic proportions' – the system of aesthetics which relates harmony in music to proportional values in architecture. Palladio's own schemes reflected the symmetrical planning he regarded as a key to the best in classical building; and it was his handling of proportion, balance and symmetry, expounded by the underlying theory, which Jones recreated in England – in an acceptably anglicized form. Inigo Jones' Queen's House at Greenwich, started four years later, and his Banqueting House in Whitehall, were quite amazingly forward looking. But it was to take both time and the development of taste before such architecture was appreciated. A

Every lamb is important on this small estate.

flirtation with the Baroque, instead, occupied the more grandiose in the ensuing half century. Although restrained by the native modesty of these islands, when compared with what was afoot on the Continent, John Vanburgh's massive Blenheim Palace near Oxford, and his Castle Howard in Yorkshire, had nonetheless rocked Englishmen back on their heels with their Baroque theatricality laced with exuberant detail. Hard-bargaining, ruddy-faced sporting squires felt ill at ease with fountains massed with statuary of the dolphins-tits-and-horses genre, and their sons, who had learned to see elegance in restraint, found themselves embarrassed by pediments bursting with glory in such heroic and uninhibited flamboyance. When, therefore, these Winchester- or Eton-educated lads came mincing home from the sunny south, they were already conditioned for a swing towards purity to be set in motion and thereafter regulated by Richard Boyle, third Earl of Burlington, the catalyst and high-priest of neo-Palladianism.

Ebberston Hall was built while the pendulum was still poised, in 1718. Its architect was Colen Campbell, first of Britain's new Palladians. Campbell's publication three years earlier of engravings depicting his most admired buildings had had an enormous impact on the rich young aesthetes hyped up on their Italian experience. Lord Burlington immediately snapped him up to complete Burlington House in Piccadilly (sacking James Gibbs, a disciple of the Baroque) before hastening back to Italy and a closer scrutiny of Palladio *in situ*. When Burlington returned in 1719, he brought with him in tow the near-illiterate, but brilliant, William Kent whom he was to groom into the most fashionable architect-designer of the age. Besides Campbell and Kent, the brood of architects clucked over by this demanding and intellectually precise patrician (himself a gifted amateur architect) included Henry Flitcroft whose slavery to his master's dicta in those years earned him the soubriquet Burlington Harry.

In many respects, Ebberston Hall exhibits in miniature the principal elements the Burlington set expounded as the gospel according to Palladio. And although in scale little more than a villa or lodge, it demonstrates the architectural principles (if not the precise features) which Colen Campbell followed in his many far larger commissions such as Stourhead in Wiltshire, Mereworth Castle, Kent, or the enormous Houghton Hall in Norfolk. Each façade is symmetrical. The lower floor is sunk beneath the main reception rooms which constitute the *piano nobile,* and this is approached by Roman steps flanked by obelisks and mounting to a terrace that spreads an apron at the entrance. Solidity is emphasized by

Gargoyle, carved in 1718, guarding the roofline of Ebberston Hall.

heavily rusticated stonework below and clean-dressed facing above the terrace level. Grotesque masks and rusticated columns lend mystery and illusions of classical antiquity to the cool depths awaiting the visitor within. From here, too, the hall is entered directly – an arrangement totally novel to the English scene – and Palladio's logical layout of rooms is employed in a balanced sequence round this central axis.

Until the end of the First War, for 500 years, West's family had owned 5,000 acres at the other side of the county in the West Riding of Yorkshire. 'Our house there was, in all honesty, already too large for the times. It had had its day as a family home, and quite properly, to my mind, had a better role awaiting it with a large steel corporation. They used it as a sort of prestige place for impressing overseas clients.' A further reason why the de Wend Fentons wanted to get out was that the estate sat plumb between the conurbations of Stockbridge and Sheffield. It became increasingly vulnerable to vandalism. 'Our tenant farmers found that stock disturbance was on the increase.' An immediate solution was to shed their less profitable moorland and reduce to about 1,000 acres. This had the effect of tightening management. 'But in the end,' he says, 'he sold up – at a mere £30 an acre – getting £30,000 for the lot.'

Having already, in 1914, acquired the more modest Ebberston Hall property, West's father moved into it in 1946; and then, after his death, West himself farmed at Ebberston. He turned 50 acres over to milk production, the balance growing cereals and feed crops. The house, meanwhile, had become uninhabitable. One of the earliest problems to be wrestled with was how to raise the funds necessary to stave off decay and prevent the Hall's eventual and perhaps inevitable collapse. And money was short. West had been away in the French Foreign Legion, sowing wilder oats than those required to support his inheritance. After being sprung from the Legion by a posse of staunch friends from home, he started farming in a serious way. Not many years passed, however, before he realized it was an up-hill battle to make a go of the property in its entirety. It became increasingly clear that the house was going to cost considerably more than the land could provide. 'I got a grant,' he recalls, 'from what was then the Ministry of Works. However, it was only a 50 per cent grant covering half the expenditure, and I had to find the other £8,000 myself. There was an awful lot to do. It meant rooting out the dry-rot, and I rebuilt the terrace and almost totally restored the garden front. We realized there was probably a bit to be made from opening to the public, and Margaret and I have been doing this now for 30 years.'

But before long, still further and larger cash injections were called for, while West's diminished farm interests were even less able than before to

Lambing time for a Jacob/Suffolk cross.

West and Margaret de Wend Fenton, and Flash.

cover his restoration bills. Accordingly, in the late '70s, West put a 3-point plan into action. This entailed selling 25 acres to cope with emergency repairs, getting the High Court to break a family trust so that he could finance a second campaign against structural decay, and applying for a local grant in the expectation of being awarded a matching grant by the Department of the Environment.

In the event, these moves were only marginally successful. West had been advised that because Ebberston was then rated at below £200 a year, he stood a good chance of winning a £6,000 local grant which, in turn, could attract £6,000 from the Department of the Environment. But the first grant was witheld and the second, consequently, not forthcoming. He was thus £12,000 down on his calculations.

The reason for this refusal to help lay in the terms in which his application had been couched. 'There's a world of difference, apparently, in the official mind, between the words 'repair' and 'restoration'. I used the wrong one. It was an expensive lesson. But the roof was made watertight, and you can see here and there where we replaced distressed stonework – mostly embellishments, mostly decorative – like some of those balusters up there, and those classical masks.'

Nor did West's High Court proceedings fulfill all their promises. Having succeeded in his bid to realize £40,000 worth of stocks and shares held in trust, he faced legal fees amounting to some £15,000 – and on top of all that a bill for capital gains tax. He was lucky, in the end, to come out with £20,000.

The de Wend Fentons are not rich. They do, however, enjoy a way of living which could be envied by many with more exacting standards and very much healthier bank balances. Life at Ebberston Hall is mercifully unconventional. As a young man, West freely admits to have been a bit on the wild side. Indeed, it is not entirely unknown for him to break out today. Those fortunate enough to find themselves within range on these occasions can testify to his enthusiasm for plunging in. Generous to a fault, irreverent, gregarious, and supercharged, seemingly, with a compulsive zest for enjoyment, he has the capacity to infect all around him – visitors, neighbouring worthies and northerners alike – with a temporary spirit of devil-may-care. 'Eee, Mr West!' they'll say, and their faces light at his approach. His mere presence can be electric. He can empty a room – or fill it, and he is loved as genuinely for his human failings as for his undoubted strengths.

At home, in the beautiful house which they have striven to save, with their animals around them and the wide landscape of Yorkshire pouring in from the horizon, life for West and Margaret de Wend Fenton is described better as rustic than rural. With the help of Jim Atkinson, now in his 77th year, who has worked on the property for more than half a century, West does his own lambing, feeds, milks and generally looks after his goats, deals with the handful of bullocks which are sold as stores, and the poultry – the peacocks and the bantams to be seen settling down to roost at night in a tree beside the coach-house. He also manages the garden himself.

To one side, below the entrance on the south front of the house, is a small area in which West puts down bedding plants at the time of the York races, in August. But it is the garden on the north side, behind the Hall, which in terms of period, pace and tranquility, is more in tune with the place. This is not a flower garden. Its historical importance derives from the fact that it is contemporary with the house, so it can therefore be looked on as unique. Still retaining some of its original elements with formal vistas, ornaments, steps and water, it is now overlaid with the informality of billowing trees and encroaching nature. Beyond the water where the black swans glide, the garden strolls off unconcernedly to join the countryside that holds it in a rising valley. In early spring snowdrops grow as they will. Meadow flowers casually mingle with tall summer grasses, and there are ferns uncurling across 18th-century masonry. For the fanciful it can take but a small breeze to enliven the scene, and the naiads and dryads which the ancients took for granted will shyly allow

The north front from the foot of the valley garden.

Bullocks on the grazing below Ebberston Hall.

themselves to be glimpsed again, for this is a setting where magic can happen.

'My grandfather used to rent Chilton House at Chilton Foliat, near Hungerford. This was designed by Inigo Jones but was later demolished by the Wills family after they acquired Littlecote. It was from there that my parents became engaged. They had gone over to Littlecote, which could be walked to easily and was in those days still the home of the Popham family. Margaret and I were married in 1955, and we've done, I suppose, what we could for this place. All houses have their own individual atmospheres. Part of the feeling about Ebberston Hall must come from its early history. Colen Campbell was commissioned by a local MP, a rather big wheel called William Thompson with the lucrative post of Master of Queen Anne's Mint. He must have also been a bit of a lad, for he built it in fact for a girl friend. Somehow Ebberston's still got that feeling about it. . . .

'We're rather out of the way up here – not enough stately homes to make it a tourist area. There's Sledmere, of course, some miles to the south. Someone once said – though I forget who now, because it's not the sort of thing you should really repeat – but this chap was looking down into the Vale and piped up rather pompously, "There's nothing between here and Sledmere". Anyhow, that apart, the holidaymakers career through to the coast. I suppose we get 2,500, say 3,000 visitors a year,

The 18th-century cascade, probably designed by Stephen Switzer.

North from the roof, to where the garden wanders casually into the countryside.

*Spring cleaning for the Easter opening: Christine Swiers (left)
and Susan Pickering.*

*'Jim Atkinson, now in his 77th year, has worked on the property
for more than half a century.'*

from Easter to the end of September. It costs them £1. You can work out the sums.'

The black, hornless lambs on the grazing below the house are a Jacob/Suffolk cross. They go to the sales in August or September. West maintains about 25 ewes which provided him with 35 lambs last season. 'Not brilliant, I grant you – but at nearly 150 a better percentage than Lochiel's!' It is quite clearly not West's intention to squeeze the maximum from his holding. 'Just look at that winter wheat over the road down there,' he says, waving from his balustraded roof towards the Vale of Pickering and a field in the middle distance striped by the sprayer. 'It may be a thing of mine, but I've made it an absolute rule that no spraying takes place on my fields.' He tackles thistles with steel. His grassland remains natural and 'unimproved'. Both West and Margaret are used to working hard, and they jog along reasonably on what they produce. 'There are always eggs. And the odd cockerel. Last week we had roast kid for lunch . . . and it did us for four days I think. Mind you, it took me four days to catch it. . . . And Flash down there – she's eleven months now – she's learning to be a sheepdog to help Jim and me out when we're past it.'

Then he turns abruptly and jerks into action. 'Let's go inside,' he calls, already striding for the ladder that descends into the house. 'See what you make of my current home-made wine. I've got gallons in the kitchen. And if we're lucky we could hit a drum that's absolutely lethal. . . .'

Hall Place

Hall Place
Kent:
Lord Hollenden

'Change? Well of course there has been change! But that's not to say the world has gone to the dogs . . .'

Alfred Houghton should know. He has been working for the Hall Place estate for 62 years and maintains that life there is as peaceful today as at any time he has known it. 'The place was a hive of activity when I arrived. We employed 18 gardeners, plus 14 estate hands, ten on the Home Farm, ten domestics, four keepers, three in our gas, water and light department, three laundry maids, two chauffeurs, the resident agent, and myself.

'On 12 December 1925,' he recalls, 'I became its first ever Estate Clerk. That was the year that the settled estate had been assigned to the second Lord Hollenden. The first baron – his father – was a terrific grandee. He had just liquidated his stud of coach horses and released four of his five grooms. The surviving one was kept on to tend the two daughters' ponies, before being eventually transferred to the estate staff. Even four years later our payroll covered 67 people. That was in 1929. Now we're down to two gardeners, two part-time indoor staff, and me. But that doesn't necessarily mean deterioration. It's merely the result of adjustment to the times.' Sitting at his desk in the modest little estate office in the outbuildings behind Hall Place, Alfred exhibits not a trace of the morbid nostalgia one might expect. Yet during his lifetime he has taken an active part in the dismantling of the machinery which had held the equilibrium on big estates across the land for centuries.

'We were perhaps better shored up against the turning tide,' he suggests, 'than those who relied solely on agriculture. Each generation here has contributed to the estate with money from the City and the family business. There was no really very pressing need to draw in our horns until comparatively late.'

Apart from closing the private laundry in 1933, and the dismissal of its staff, major changes were staved off for another two decades. When they came, most were pre-empted by the War or its aftermath. 'Take our gas, water and light department. We used to pump water from our own well at the waterworks to supply the mansion and our houses and cottages in the village. Modernization was forced on us because the waterworks was bombed. That was in early 1942. We had two gasometers there as well, and generated our own electricity. Until we were put on to mains supply, these all served the mansion and our village property. Even so, although its days were numbered by the 1940s, it was not until 1964 that we pensioned off the last of our gas, water and light staff.'

The core of the estate lies around the village of Leigh, a little to the west of Tonbridge. Leigh is every inch an estate village. Even the rash of later building fails to dilute its plummy flavour. There is a look about Leigh of self-esteem and dependability, and of unabashed Victorian confidence in having plumped for Elizabethan as its architectural model. No two buildings are the same, yet they hang together with strong family features inherited from the rustic *cottage orné*. Fine carved brickwork is a notable feature, particularly of the chimney stacks which are massive and ornately stepped. Then there are jettied gables, heavy with timber, tile-hung walls

Sixty two years on the Hall Place estate, Alfred Houghton (right) and Gordon Hollenden contemplate the future.

Jettied gables, heavy with timber, give an air of dependability to the village of Leigh which was central to the Victorian ethos.

and leaded windows. These hark back with pride to some legendary England which in truth perhaps never existed but which – like Leigh – was central to the ethos of Victoria's time and was to last as long and as decently as her Empire.

It comes therefore as no great surprise to learn that the roofs, now tiled, were originally thatched, and that village and estate date from 1870. In that year a Kentish farmer called Baily sold 398 acres and a modest country house to the hosiery manufacturer Samuel Morley. Morley, then 61, epitomized the successful magnate of his day. He was the second generation to control the family company J. & R. Morley which had started in the Midlands at the end of the 18th century and was the most successful of its kind in the country. Having made his millions from manufacturing stockings and underwear, Morley found himself with the leisure to indulge his qualities of rectitude and benevolence. The opportunity was provided by his Hall Place property in the lush and leafy heart of Kent. Elected MP for Nottingham and Bristol, he was concerned with moves against slavery, and for the improvement of factory and working conditions. He was Nonconformist and teetotal (in each case sufficiently fervently to expect no less from those who worked for him), and out of Nonconformist principle he was to refuse the offer of a peerage. At Leigh, and the neighbouring village of Hildenborough, Morley's benevolence showed itself in the way he lavished his very considerable fortune on providing for the community on his newly-acquired acres the most advanced amenities that money could buy.

Having acquired his agricultural estate, Samuel Morley decided that the house was not what he wanted. Accordingly, in 1871, he pulled it down and commissioned a new Hall Place 100 yards from the site – a massive red-brick Gothic structure befitting the wealth and status of its owner. Next he proceeded to integrate Leigh village with the estate. This he achieved by building a chapel, a school and the Village Hall, building two squares – Forge Square and Leigh Square – and a number of other houses and cottages, and providing mains water and gas to the village. 'Samuel Morley's village,' Alfred Houghton declares, 'was half a century in advance of its time.' He also laid out Leigh Green, the dominant open feature, and provided the allotments at the end of the village.

Money was not stinted. The accounts of George Myers & Sons, builders of Lambeth, for the years 1871 to 1874 record £54,365 in connection with work on the new Hall Place and a further £8,551 on its stable buildings. In addition, £2,290 was spent on the terrace and yard walls, £1,143 on a tank on its mound and a fountain in the grounds, and £3,071 on other work around the property.

North-east from the roof over the 'green and leafy heart of Kent'.

LEFT: *The carriage house entrance.*

On Samuel Morley's death in 1886, the property passed to his eldest son, Samuel Hope-Morley, who was to be created first Baron Hollenden in 1912. Because the village had traditionally been Church of England, the people now forsook the Chapel – no doubt with some relief – and returned to the bosom of the Church. A handful remained faithful, however, and for these Samuel Hope-Morley built a second chapel at Hildenborough.

In his day, the first Lord Hollenden would have been one of the 'heavy swells'. Alfred Houghton recalls him with a relish he finds hard to conceal. 'He was a very substantial man, with sound financial acumen. A director of the Bank of England, he kept a large stable, drove a four-in-hand, and maintained a large yacht. He supported the Church and the village in every possible way. Under his reign the estate expanded to more than three times its original extent, from just under 400 acres to 1,400 acres. Lord Hollenden also loved his shooting. In 1916 he rented the shooting of Penshurst Place across the fields – just over 1,000 acres south of the Medway – at £125 a year, and a further 1,700 acres north of the river at £300 a year. Eight keepers were employed to cover the two shoots. Those were great times. The resident agents were important men, respected – even feared – on the properties they controlled. In our immediate neighbourhood such men were employed at Fairlawn by the Cazalets . . . Hever Castle by the Astors . . . Somerhill at Tonbridge where the D'Avigdor Goldsmids lived . . . at Penshurst . . . and of course here on the Hall Place estate. The shooting agreement with the Lords De L'Isle and Dudley didn't terminate until 31 January 1956.'

Four years before Lord Hollenden's death, the estate was assigned to his son Geoffrey Hope-Morley who moved to Hall Place in 1925. Geoffrey's influence is to be seen especially in the gardens. Still outstanding today, in the years before the War they were the scene of continuing expansion and experiment. 'If he hadn't died,' laughs his nephew, the present Lord Hollenden, 'they would probably reach as far as Tonbridge now.'

The view from the house is dominated by a 14-acre lake, a sheet of water with its wild and resident wildfowl and three lakeside bridges which Geoffrey built. Nearer the house, a formal, terraced Italian-type garden was laid out by the estate's founder. Geoffrey Hollenden was to improve and keep this to a very high standard, with help of his 18 gardeners. The property is distinguished throughout by his marvellous specimen trees, many of them now half a century on. It is not without significance, perhaps, that a larger workforce was employed in Geoffrey's

Fourteen acres of water, with trees and wildfowl, dominate the view from Hall Place.

gardens than to staff his house which nobody could call small. In the event, following a fire in 1940, one-third of the mansion had to be demolished, yet its size was still daunting enough to cause the next Lord Hollenden to stipulate more drastic reductions still before he would consider moving in.

One of the first things Alfred Houghton did as estate clerk was to prepare the first tax claims for farm losses and estate maintenance. 'This showed the keen financial control maintained by the second Lord.' When the resident agent left in 1940, Alfred took over his duties, which he continues to this day. 'Fifty years ago,' he claims, 'almost all of the village one way or another was involved in the estate. They occupied our houses and cottages, worked in the various departments of the estate and provided the domestic staff, and in the season acted as beaters at Hall Place and at Penshurst Place.' There was a strong feeling of unity. Geoffrey Hollenden, for his part, threw himself no less wholeheartedly into the life of the village. When they were needed, he would provide additional cottages, as at Home Farm and the entrance to Prices Farm. He took an active part in village activities, and perhaps in gratitude for this, in 1948, he made the village a gift of their green which his grandfather had laid out. Geoffrey Hollenden severed Leigh Green from the Hall Place estate and handed it over through the Parish Council.

In 1952 he went further for Geoffrey created a charitable trust which he named the Morley Trust. To this trust he made over the Village Hall and Institute (now occupied by the local branch of the British Legion), as well as Leigh Free Church, the Scouts' headquarters, the allotments, and the chapel at Hildenborough – all complete with their fixtures and chattels. He explained at the time of the hand-over how he had spent many happy hours in the Village Hall at dances, dinners and concerts, and attended 'hundreds and hundreds' of meetings in one or other of these buildings during the previous half century. 'Now' he continued, 'I want to feel that their future is assured.' In 1984, 32 years later, the Parish Council became the owner of the Village Hall and Institute. Less happily, meanwhile, the Free Church closed for lack of support and was sold to a local builder and burned out. Today, too, the future remains uncertain for the allotments. In April 1987, the Scout headquarters and the Chapel were handed over to new charitable trusts.

When Alfred Houghton was newly appointed, the property had numbered 79 buildings spread across the parishes of Leigh and Hildenborough. Their total rent in 1930 was £1,879-2s-9d. By the 1950s, the whole basis of economics in the country had changed, and problems were accumulating for Hall Place. The buildings were becoming increasingly

Lord and Lady Hollenden . . Peter . . . and daffodils.

'*You might say that the summer at Hall Place went right on into autumn.*'

Gordon Hollenden's farming partner is Colin Bastable, at home with his Friesian cows at Leigh Park Farm.

'Their aim is 150 calves a season.'

Home Farm, now tenanted, reflects the same 'plummy', rustic flavour that pervades Morley's model village.

hard to maintain, while the future of the estate itself was made problematic by the high rate of Estate Duty. By conveying his public buildings to the charitable trust, Lord Hollenden had opened the door to a more general shedding of estate property. If it was to remain a recognizable entity, more of its less profitable parts would have to go.

In 1958 Geoffrey Hollenden purchased the reversion to property of Gordon Hope-Morley (his nephew, the present peer) which included 37 houses and cottages, two shops and the waterworks. As these became vacant they were sold. The estate also moved from holding land in hand to leasing it to tenants. In 1966, its 324-acre Home Farm was let by tender, and within two years the estate maintenance staff of five was made redundant. Next, between 1969 and 1971, the Tonbridge By-Pass arrived, taking more than 20 acres from the Home Farm and severing a further seven from the rest of the estate. The latter remnant was sold. Finally, in 1976, the year before Geoffrey Hollenden's death, it was decided to sell the first important slice of the property – Price's Farm House; and Lower Street Farm House was sold in 1979. Three years before this first farmhouse sale however, in 1973, the estate had been assigned to Gordon Hope-Morley and consequently disentailed.

Gordon succeeded his uncle in 1977 and within two years revolutionized its management structure. Hall Place estate has been slimmed down from 1,400 to 1,277 acres, all of which are let. The formerly labour-intensive gardens are now mainly shrubs – 'no bedding stuff', as Gordon puts it. The Deer Park's traditional herd of 60 fallow deer was dispersed in 1963 to lift the prohibitive cost of renewing the 6ft high fencing. Estate labour has been progressively shed, and all village properties sold apart from those which belong to Geoffrey's widow. However, the restructuring effected by Gordon, the third Lord Hollenden, introduced a form of partnership to the management of the farms.

Hall Place Farms Partnership was formed in 1979, the partners being Gordon Hollenden and his neighbours Roy and Colin Bastable. Essentially, the arrangement was that the Bastables provided a hop farm, agricultural land and woodland totalling some 320 acres, while Lord Hollenden provided his 180-acre Lower Street Farm and nearly 100 acres known as Deer Park, Rookery and Cherry Orchard. The Bastables also included 411 acres comprising Leigh Park and Prices Farm which they hold as tenants of Lord Hollenden. Over the next few years two further smallish properties were added; the 80 acres of Paddock Wood provided by the Bastables were sold, and Salmons Farm of 143 acres was bought and added to the partnership. The Home Farm is still leased and remains the property of Lord Hollenden.

*Pheasant in hand, Donald Hallett – first-class shot
and the last of a great line of estate keepers.*

The estate's serious activities are dairy farming, sheep, hops and woodland. Its fun activity is shooting.

In recent years its five dairy herds have been reduced to the one which is centred on Leigh Park Farm. Gordon explains how their aim is a production level of 150 calves a season, some to be fattened and sold at two years. 'The great problem with dairy is the milk quotas. They lay down how much you are allowed to produce. Exceed the quota and a levy is imposed.' All told, these flat green pastures support between 500 and 600 cattle for the partnership. Calving takes place between August and January. When they are due, the cows are given ten days in the shed, in a maternity ward atmosphere, sweet with hay and personal attention. 'Autumn is our busy time. The herdsman and his wife do all the calving, and at the moment he is milking, I think, 140. There's another 100 beef cattle down at Lower Street Farm where they are self fed on silage. In summer they are grazed on outlying areas of the estate.'

In autumn, lambs are bought for fattening and selling in March; and early September sees the hops being picked, after which they are dried and sold to the Hop Marketing Board. And at the same time the partnership might be cutting maize, or drilling corn on Lower Street.

The woodland management revolves round a cycle of coppicing chestnut and hazel. This recurs every 13 to 16 years. Gordon uses the old Kentish word 'cant', to describe the two to three acres that are worked at a time by the partnership or the contractors they bring in. It is all very gentle. Alfred was right. Life on this property appears to be as peaceful today as ever.

The first shoot syndicate was formed in 1962, in which Geoffrey Hollenden reserved three guns for himself. Hall Place shoot covered 1,400 acres, and for a few years an additional 330 acres were rented from neighbouring farms. On Geoffrey's departure in 1973, a syndicate was formed by his friends, the rent being 5s an acre which came to £350 per annum.

'I started to shoot,' Gordon recalls, 'it must have been in 1926, when I was ten or eleven, in Scotland. It has always given me the greatest of pleasure, although I'm not interested these days in enormous bags and so on. Anyhow, the shoot here reverted to me in February 1987, and I was delighted to take it back into my own hands. You might as well enjoy your last few years. . . We've got one keeper. That's Donald Hallett, a young man of about 30 who lost his arm some eight years ago. He spends his non-keeping time as a self-employed carpenter, and incidentally, is a first-class shot.'

With his shooting, therefore, and relieved of the day-to-day practicalities of farming and management, Gordon Hollenden has time for enjoyment. As its the last chairman, too, he sold the family business to Courtalds. 'What other areas do I derive pleasure from? Well, gardens and gardening for a start. I am a trustee of the Chelsea Physic Garden – indeed at the moment am heavily engaged in trying to raise £1 million for them. It may seem a far cry from this garden, in that it's a scholarly collection of age and considerable importance, but I find that I am deeply involved. In a way you might say that now Hall Place is organized, I've got a job to help the Physic Garden to face the future with confidence.'

Sark

Sark

Channel Islands:
Michael Beaumont, Esquire,
The Seigneur of Sark

You can't fly to Sark. That's unless you're The Queen Mother and are dropping in by helicopter. For you and me it means a flight to Guernsey, with a stop-over at St Peter's Port where the ferry leaves from. Apart from the bar prices – which are gratifyingly cheap – the way of life here appears little different from the mainland. Sharply suited young men with 'executive' briefcases slide in and out of taxis at the airport. Traffic whizzes along a sea-front lined with Georgian and Victorian buildings, and behind it are found chain stores with facias familiar from a hundred high streets at home. Then the hotel bar is held ransom by the Rugby club, hull down in revelry; and when that pack has left it is possible to detect enough different accents to chart the demographic face of the United Kingdom. Guernsey, in short, a Sterling island, is stamped with the hallmarks of sophistication.

Sark, however, is still to come. And it is something very different indeed. For the past five days it has been blowing great guns, so boats have been unable to make the crossing. But now with a forecast of clear skies and sub-zero temperatures, and the east wind moderating from force eight to six, the *Bon Marin de Serk* can almost certainly be counted on for the seven-mile passage in the morning. The boat is scheduled to make three round trips a week – weather permitting. A major fascination of any small island is that there's always a chance of getting stuck there.

Sark is the fourth largest of the Channel Islands, the low-lying, fertile, granite humps clustered in the angle formed by Brittany and the Cherbourg peninsula. Eighty miles or so due south of Hampshire, but barely twenty miles within clear view from Normandy, geographically they are more a fragment of France than of England. Indeed, until the Conquest, they were, in a political sense, as part of the duchy of Normandy. But on William of Normandy's winning the throne in 1066, Sark and the rest of the Islands found themselves united with his English realm. Through some happy quirk of history, moreover, the Channel Islands remained English after 1214, when King John lost the lion's share of his duchy to France. Frequently referred to as our oldest colony, they remain the sole vestige of the duchy of Normandy surviving under the British crown.

As the *Bon Marin* plunges through the swell, the silhouette of Sark coming up on the right shows it as an unapproachable plateau raised high above the sea on a curtain of daunting cliffs. Its shape on the map is that of an inverted head and body, an upside-down hour-glass measuring three-and-a-half miles from north to south and perhaps one-and-a-half miles across at its widest. The map also reveals that the southern portion, the head, is virtually a separate island. The two parts – Little Sark and Great Sark – are joined by a neck two-thirds of the way down, which serves as a natural causeway. This is known as La Coupée. Hardly wider than an ox-cart, it runs for about 150 yards, and because the whole island is lifted 300 feet above the waves, La Coupée affords quite an experience for those who like to flirt with vertigo from behind the safety of a hand-rail.

Until the late Middle Ages, the island was populated by the descendants of its pre-Conquest inhabitants. But life was never to be tranquil for long. Sark became the prey of marauders from both sides of the Channel. In the reign of

Hardly wider than an ox-cart, Le Coupée runs for about 150 yards. Following the Liberation, this raised causeway was refurbished by the Royal Engineers using the labour of German prisoners-of-war.

The whole island is raised high above the sea on a curtain of daunting cliffs.

King John it was seized and held by the noted pirate Eustache le Moine, and it frequently came under attack from the French as well. Most prudent Sarkeses, looking for an easier existence, made off for the larger islands, although Guernsey itself became the target of the French in the reigns of Edward I and Edward VI. By 1372 even the venerable Priory of Saint Magloire, which had been founded on Sark around the year 565, was finally abandoned as untenable; and thereafter for the best part of 200 years 'Sercq' was very largely given over to a motley collection of robbers and brigands. A brief period of French occupation in the mid–16th century might perhaps have afforded the island a certain respite, but for the remainder of the Islands, the proximity of the French, coupled to the continuing threat of raiders, was a festering thorn in the side.

This state of affairs persisted until Tudor times. Then, in the early 1560s, a certain Helier de Carteret decided that enough was enough. De Carteret was the premier Seigneur of Jersey, the largest of the Channel Islands, and he combined both vision and action. First he sailed out and colonized Sark with men hand-picked from his existing lands. This effectively put paid to further use by either pirates or the French. Then he petitioned the Queen, Elizabeth I, with the proposal that she should allow him to add Sark to his lands. Elizabeth agreed, and in 1565 she granted de Carteret a charter stating that de Carteret should hold Sark from the Crown as a fief – a kind of perpetual leasehold – with all the rights and privileges of a feudal lord. He would be its first Seigneur. The charter also stated that de Carteret should have 40 men capable of bearing muskets, to 'keep the island free of the Queen's enemies', and that he should provide her with knight's service in perpetuity, a fee which would cost him at the rate of one man for a 20th part of each year. That the organization set up by Helier de Carteret has survived essentially unchanged to this day is testimony no less to his own administrative flair than to the grasp of practicalities enjoyed by Elizabeth.

'Obligation and tithe, as opposed to law and money, are the main distinctions between feudalism and what came after.' Michael Beaumont, heir and grandson of the celebrated Dame of Sark, has been Seigneur since her death in 1974. 'In many ways,' he maintains, 'we are still a feudal community. Naturally, I no longer stand in the fields at harvest time and watch every tenth sheaf being pitched onto my *dîme* cart. Nor do I despatch a Sarkese to Windsor for a couple of weeks' military service a year. These have been translated into the language of money. My annual fee these days to the Queen is – if I'm right – about £1.79. And the tithe cart – the old *dîme* cart parked out there in the Battery – became obsolete the day the combine harvester arrived. That was in 1957. And incidentally, in our Sarkese patois we pronounce it "deem" in the French way.'

Diana and Michael Beaumont in their garden on Sark.

Michael Beaumont is as conscious of the responsibilities he has inherited as Seigneur as he is of his traditional – if vestigial – privileges. The island is barely two square miles in area. Helier de Carteret divided his fief into 40 holdings – 39 of which he leased in perpetuity to his men-at-arms, the 40th which he kept for himself. Besides his tithe, his one-tenth of their produce, the Seigneur and his successors reserved their tenants' obligation to provide one (in some cases two) armed men should there be a need for defence. To this day de Carteret's 40 tenements form the basis of Sark's agricultural units. 'Farming in fact would cease to be economic if those landholdings were ever to be diminished. They only run to 30 acres apiece, and a second charter of 1611 expressly forbade their being broken up. Nowadays I combine two tenements, giving me 60 acres which I lease to a neighbouring farmer. But the original boundaries have remained very much the same, and the names of each tenement still apply and cover the same ground as in de Carteret's day.'

The original landing had been up at the north end of the island, until Creux Harbour was built in Elizabethan times under the flanks of the eastern cliffs. Creux is thus sheltered from the prevailing winds. But when the seas are piling up from a steady north-easter, a landfall here can be problematical – as it can be, too, at Masseline's quayside a couple of hundred yards round the headland. From each of these harbours the approach to the hinterland is literally through the cliff by way of a rock-hewn tunnel. These, in turn, lead to the unmetalled Harbour Hill which slices up for half a mile to the plateau commanding the island's spine. There are no cars on Sark. Its well-maintained roads are innocent of tarmac. There is no need for traffic lights or parking regulations and all the horrors that these can spawn. The air is clean, and although the *Bon Marin's* arrival will be greeted by a flotilla of tractors – each with a trailer to carry up the eagerly awaited mail, provisions and passengers from the outside world – when the visitor steps ashore, he may well feel that he has stepped from the 20th into the 19th century – and, paradoxically, from the Old World to the New.

Passing the island's post office, its church, the prison and school, a run of one-storey shops and Colonial-style bungalows, the white dust ribbon neatly lined with trees leads to the gates of La Seigneurie. This is a slightly mad-looking granite pile dominated by a Victorian tower. It is the home of Michael and Diana Beaumont. Probably it is at this point that the visitor makes an essential adjustment: the fact that there is no traffic to speak of means that there is also no need for a conventional drive. Instead, the visitor approaches the house on foot. Then, as the house finally reveals itself through a sheltering screen of holm oaks, a flutter of pure white fantail pigeons will clap the air and wheel round the treetops before settling again to peck the ground at the foot of their *colombier*. The visitor will have

*Simple agriculture still helps the Sarkese to earn a living
from their ancient 30-acre tenements.*

Bon Marin de Serk, *having off-loaded vital provisions at Maseline.*

Main street on Sark.

experienced one at least of the *droits de seigneur* maintained by Michael Beaumont. As lord of Sark, he alone on the island has the traditional right to own a dovecote.

La Seigneurie has clearly had a chequered career. Helier de Carteret and his successors lived in the Elizabethan house which he built in the centre of the island. Still called Le Manoir, it stands half a mile or so away to the south. But in 1730 the family sold their fief to a certain Suzanne Le Pelley. The Le Pelleys had, for a century or more, occupied the tenement known as La Perronerie in a house they had built close to the present Seigneurie. One of the original 40 houses dating from the years after the re-colonization, it eventually fell into disrepair and was demolished in the 1920s. No-one knows for certain when today's Seigneurie was built although a date incized above a fireplace suggests 1675. It is, however, established that the panelling was introduced in 1732 when the windows were enlarged in line with the fashion. That original portion of the house is incorporated in the south-facing front of the much larger building which has grown around it. Meanwhile, a smaller and quite separate house was put up close to the north-west of La Seigneurie, and soon afterwards the two were merged together to form one sprawling and far less comprehensible dwelling when the intervening space was infilled.

The next development dates from 1854. The Seigneur of the time was the Rev. W. T. Collings, Michael's great-great-grandfather, and it was he who added the enormous drawing room and the tower which is at the same time

Michael Beaumont's seigneurial colombier. *He alone on the island has the right to own a dovecote.*

the chief feature and the dottiest element of this extraordinary mansion. Michael is staunchly loyal to the drawing room, with its massive, over-elaborate fireplace and lofty Victorian plate-glass windows. 'Perfect,' he maintains, 'for any official entertaining that's needed.' And the tower? 'Well, come up and see the view. I think you'll find it worth the climb. . . . There's Guernsey to our west. And Jersey you can see just east by south. Now over there, that's France, that long line of coast which it looks as if you could reach out and touch. The little town of Carteret, where the first Seigneur's family came from, is tucked in just behind that southern headland, and les Pieux lies dead opposite us, a couple of kilometers inland.'

The tower is a good vantage point from which to look down on the chapel. Some medieval masonry incorporated there has inevitably prompted extravagant claims of antiquity. One of these links it with the long-abandoned Priory, a theory strengthened by the fact that a genuine stretch of Priory wall has survived a stone's throw from the house. But the chapel is almost certainly a modern affair. It probably dates from no earlier than the 18th century. And if this is the case, we may also be sure that it was built as much in a spirit of defiance as piety.

Suzanne Le Pelley was not the first and certainly won't be the last *grande dame* to fall out with her parish priest. Few, however, have the temerity to pursue their vendettas to such bizarre extremes. Suzanne's methods of conducting a row was to lead as far as her excommunication. Embattled with the island's wretched pastor, quarrelling with him openly and with scant restraint, there came a point when she cast about to arm herself with the ultimate weapon of offence. This she presently recognized hanging conveniently on a nail. Taking the key from the wall, Suzanne turned it on the priest. She locked him out of his own church.

When the wheel turned, it was Suzanne Le Pelley who found herself debarred from public worship. And this deprivation served as the origin of the little building we are looking at. Far from being chastened, Sark's high-handed Dame determined to go it alone. She would worship as she pleased, and this she did, in her own new private seigneurial chapel.

An intriguing footnote illustrates the repetition of history. Two centuries later, another Dame of Sark, although neither as headstrong perhaps nor as extreme as Suzanne, was to echo her predecessor's disdain for her clergy. She, too, had periods of friction with those dedicated to the cure of souls on Sark.

From the tower one also looks down into the Battery area with its scattering of artillery pieces. Those 18th-century iron cannon came from a privateer in the service of one of the Beaumonts' not so law-abiding forebears. In stark contrast are a First World War mortar and a field gun

*Innocent of tarmac, the white dust roads have neither street lights nor parking
regulations and the horrors that these can spawn.*

'The Le Pelleys embarked on an ill-fated silver mining venture close to
the tip of Little Sark.'

left on Sark by the Germans after the second. But the *pièce de resistance,* and the most elegant on display, is the great bronze cannon that has been on the island for more than 400 summers. The inscription on the barrel tells the tale: 'Don de sa Majesté la Royne Elizabeth au Seigneur de Sercq A.D. 1572'.

In the opposite direction, beyond Suzanne's chapel, the geometrical layout of the formal garden catches one's attention. This is one of the finest gardens of its type in the Channel Islands. Sheltered by high walls from winds off the sea, its planning and planting were largely the work of the late Dame Sibyl Hathaway, DBE. 'She was a great gardener and a remarkable woman, my grandmother. During the occupation in the War it was very largely due to her that the islanders managed to survive. She was totally fearless. And she would stand no nonsense. First, of course, she spoke fluent German and knew the way they ticked. And second, she was, I am afraid, a terrific snob. She understood only too well that the Germans were too – and she played on that knowledge to the island's advantage.'

Michael Beaumont's family acquired the seigneurity from the Le Pelleys in much the same way as Dame Suzanne Le Pelley had bought it from the de Carterets. In the early 19th century, the Le Pelleys embarked on an ill-fated silver mining venture. The remains of their workings are still to be seen close to the southern tip of Little Sark. 'Like so many people convinced of ultimate success, they sank in far too much money for little return, and while the wretched business dragged on and on they ran up enormous debts. A lot of the money was lent by my family, who were called Collings and lived on Guernsey. Eventually when the time came to call it in there was nothing left, so in 1852 we foreclosed.'

The first Collings to be Seigneur was the clergyman who Victorianized the house. His son, who succeeded him, appears to have been a convivial soul with a tendency to go out 'on a spree'. On the death of this Seigneur, however, there being no male heir, the privileges and duties fell on the capable shoulders of his daughter Sibyl. Sibyl Collings' first husband was Dudley Beaumont – Michael's grandfather –who died in 1918 from the 'flu epidemic which swept Europe on the heels of the Armistice. Some years later she married a second time, to become Sibyl Hathaway. For many years of course, in the seigneurial sense, Sibyl had been known as the Dame of Sark. After the War, however, she was also created a Dame of the British Empire. This introduced into her style of address a distinct but happily coincidental use of that same distinguished Norman word for 'lady'. Her husband Robert Hathaway dying before her, Sibyl remained on the Island as a widow until 1974 when she herself died at the splendid age of 90. By that time, her eldest son by Dudley Beaumont had also died, leaving the seignieury and the fief to fall to her grandson Michael.

After studying engineering at Loughborough College, Michael Beaumont became an authority on small aircraft, and he fetched up near Bristol on guided weapon installation. In 1956 he had married another Channel Islander, Diana La Trobe-Bateman. Their oldest son Christopher is now a Captain in the Royal Engineers; Anthony, their younger, practices medicine in a London hospital.

Before the War, Michael used to visit his grandmother on Sark. Naturally, however, those pleasures were denied him during the German occupation. The islanders in those hard years were only saved from starvation by the Red Cross food parcels. 'Give them their due though,' maintains Diana Beaumont, 'the Germans at no time attempted to cut these off – not even towards the end when they were starving themselves. I remember Michael's grandmother recalling that period. About the Germans she certainly entertained no illusions. Yet her comment, on this question of food, was clearly objective: 'Thank God,' she commented – and she meant it seriously – 'thank God our occupiers weren't French!'' Diana recalls, too, how after an abortive Commando raid the Germans sowed the clifftops with land-mines. This was disastrous for the Sarkeses, for it cut them off from the one source of meat that had been reasonably available. They could no longer kill rabbits in the clifftop scrub. 'The Dame got through the War on lobster. She swore that after it was over she'd never touch one again. And she didn't. She stuck to her guns.'

One can hardly overlook the personality of the old Dame of Sark who had such an impact on all who knew her. Legend has already embroidered reminiscence. Books have been written, and a successful play produced, about that colourful, gallant and wilful woman and they by no means over-emphasize her courage and determination. From the outset the Dame demonstrated to the occupying forces that her little community on Sark was an organized set-up, perfectly capable of managing its own affairs. Approaches to the populace could properly only be made through her. When the Germans therefore came up to the Seigneurie to consult or to arbitrate with the Dame, she received them from the commanding position of her own authoritative home, her ancient seignieury, and unquestionable moral superiority. The Com-

Dame Sibyl Hathaway was largely responsible for the present layout and planting of La Seigneurie's extensive walled garden.

mando raid (in reality a practice run) caused the Germans to round up any Englishmen still on the island and to pack them off for internment in Germany. Among these was Sibyl's husband Robert. On another occasion, Teutonic logic came up with the timetable notion that fishing was to be permitted only during certain prescribed hours. For the order to be promulgated, Dame Sibyl's signature was needed. Her scorn was magnificent. Had they no understanding of the movements of fish? Didn't they recognize factors such as weather and tides, and how these could stop boats from leaving Creux Harbour . . . and prevent them returning within the hours set down? More soundly based, and more forcefully argued than the Germans', Dame Sibyl's persuasion prevailed.

Sark is the Crown's smallest Dependency. It has a population of about 550. Only 100 years ago English was introduced as a second language in its schools, and even in the present Seigneur's time there were a couple of islanders who spoke only their patois. The insularity of the Sarkeses is jealously guarded.

'We have no divorce on the Island,' explains Micahel Beaumont. 'And we don't want it, either. The two main reasons have to do with economics and inheritance. Allow divorce laws in and there's always a danger of property getting divided. A Court might even go so far as to rule on who should inherit, who a property should be passed to. So we not only don't have divorce, but the islanders have quite positively thrown the idea out – although of course we recognize it as a fact of life elsewhere. Property orders on our island would be the thin end of the wedge. Ram it home and it would spell the death of profitable farming. In the same way that we are a Dependency and not part of the United Kingdom, we're also, mercifully, not full – only associate – members of the EEC. In other small communities membership has all but killed off agriculture. Look at the Scilly Islands. How, for example, could a man farming 30 acres afford the luxury of a registered slaughterhouse? He'd never make a profit on his stock. Our way may be old-fashioned. But for us it works. It works – and also it's cheap.'

Keeping costs down is greatly helped by the fact that Sark levies no income tax. Yet the most casual glance will show that its roads are well maintained, the harbours sound, and that its children go to school where they are presumably educated as well as the rest of us. So where does the island's revenue come from?

'We must be almost alone in the world in that our economy is totally divorced from the wealth of our citizens.' Michael outlines how two separate accounts provide the island's funds. The larger is the general revenue account. Currently running at about £150,000 a year, this is kept

Rugged cliffland on the west side of the island.

going principally on the small excise duty levelled on alcohol and tobacco, and on a landing tax on visitors. 'The general fund covers all capital and maintenance expenditure and also the salaries of the island employees. So apart from drinks and cigarettes, which are still cheaper than on Guernsey, the island ticks over on visitors. They pay our doctor's salary, which is £5,000 a year – tax-free as you'll remember – and our three teachers who get £15,000 between them. The general fund will be drawn on to help, for example, a particularly bright child who needs further education on the mainland beyond his parents' means. The island ambulance and fire service also come under this umbrella, as do expenditure on, say, roadside tree planting and the individual clumps of trees we are planning to establish.'

The second fund runs to about £50,000 a year and is devoted to the welfare of the elderly and needy. 'Its income is the small property and capital tax we indulge in. This is all very friendly. We sit down once a year and solemnly decide among ourselves how much we are going to tax each other. We base this not on our income because our income, whatever it is, is usually kept rather dark. Our far more charming way of tax assessment is to base it on our wealth as perceived by the others.'

Besides being self financing, Sark is also self-governing, and in almost every aspect of its legislature the Seigneur is involved. 'The Court of Chief Pleas, as our parliament's called, was established by Helier de Carteret. The head of each of his 40 tenements was a member, and he appointed five jurats to administer justice. Chief Pleas also includes twelve Deputies, elected triennially, who represent later arrivals without an interest in a tenement.' In the old days, public works such as road building and maintenance was enforced by imposing a *corvée*. This obliged each man, with his horse and cart, to provide labour for a certain number of days a year. 'I am afraid the *corvée*, like my fee to the Crown and the old tithing system, has now come down to paying out money. And de Carteret's jurats were stood down in 1675. Justice these days lies with a lay magistrate called the Seneschal. He is assisted by the Prevot, a kind of sheriff who sees that the orders of the court are obeyed, and by the Greffier who acts as clerk of court. Each of these august figures is appointed by the Seigneur, and the Seneschal is the chairman of the Court of Chief Pleas.' Chief Pleas can only sit in the presence of the Seigneur or his deputy. Michael's experience of sitting there with his grandmother was an essential part of his training. All items have to have the Seigneur's approval, although his veto, should it be exercized, has a 21 days limit.

Even more enlightened is how the Sarkeses run their police. Every man on the island has his chance for a year. Responsibility for law and order rests with the Constable and his assistant the Vingtenier, so called because originally there was one for every 20 households. These are both honorary posts, elected annually by the Chief Pleas. 'Our little island prison,' says Michael, 'is not often used, except for foreigners who have over-indulged. And luckily there's a three-day limit to our holding them there. Bank Holidays are the worst, when the tourists are in spate, so we borrow a regular policeman from Guernsey. But you must understand our powers are not unlimited. Serious cases are referred to Guernsey, there's always a right of appeal to the Royal Court on that island.'

Although the Seigneur of Sark's feudal powers have been whittled down over the centuries to an almost constitutional level, he still performs an important role in the administration. The Seigneur is responsible to the Crown – in the person of the Lieutenant Governor in Guernsey – for the well-being of the island and the islanders. And he still retains a number of enviable privileges. The Seigneur's permission is needed whenever a tenement is bought and sold. For this he exacts his *treizième*, which amounts to one-thirteenth of the purchase price. He maintains his sole right to the island's minerals; to flotsam and jetsam; to mills and milling, and to streams. And besides being the only Islander allowed his *colombier*, Michael Beaumont alone can keep a bitch.

The island's fire-fighting force, with its tractor-drawn pump, prepares for its monthly practice.

East from Le Creux – the rock-strewn waters of the Channel.

Landholding is unique not only because it can't be broken up. Neither can it be left by will. Unless it is sold (the Seigneur taking his cut) it must pass by inheritance through male primogeniture. Similarly, islanders may only will one-third of their personal property. A third must go to the surviving spouse, and another third to the children. When divorce laws were drafted in Guernsey, the Sarkeses were adamant in their rejection. Part of the reason, as Michael has pointed out, has to do with survival on the produce of their finite acreage. But in part it also reflects their respect for a tradition which they know has worked since Tudor times. Should you ask if the young tend to drift to the mainland, a Sarkese will give you a look as if you've lost your senses. 'No, we don't leave the island,' they laugh. 'This is our home, and we love it. It's open and uncluttered, and there's no crime to speak of. It's almost impossible for a foreigner to get a landholding in Sark, so we carry on as a community in the way we know is best.'

Then you ask – how can you not? – the inevitable question to be posed in a place where divorce is unknown. And for the first time you'll achieve not an evasion but a gulp and the briefest of pauses while diplomacy is summoned. 'Well of course people have affairs! Same as anywhere else. Except here, you understand, the children – uhm – well the kids are for ever in and out of each other's houses. It's all very natural. They treat us all as their parents, and we treat the children as if they were all our own.'

It was Dame Sibyl Hathaway – the greatest of all Sarkeses since Helier de Carteret – who insisted on driving through married women's rights. Before she forced the issue, married women on Sark (as opposed to girls or widows) were entitled to own neither property nor money. Yet when discussing life and love with these ladies of Sark, it would clearly be ludicrous to sound them out on the question of second-class citizenship.

And when the *Bon Marin de Serk* has furrowed the rock-strewn waters and you stand again on Guernsey, it is impossible to avoid a sense of loss. Analyse this and you find you have shed preconceptions and standards which Sark has quietly exposed as false. Can these jostling cars, you wonder, those belching chimneys, can those property ads, the tourist shops, those credit card-flicking businessmen – can these seriously indicate civilization? Before departure they had seemed the hallmarks of sophistication. On return it is hard to duck the suspicion that a more apposite word is second-rate.

Beaulieu

Beaulieu

Hampshire:
Lord Montagu of Beaulieu

Ask a random sample of people to name the first stately home that comes to mind. The chances are that Beaulieu will be the runaway winner. Close behind, Woburn and Longleat will cross the line straining for joint second place. But none of the others – the Chatsworths, the Blenheims, the Castle Howards and Ragleys – will even be in the same race. And the reason for this is not just that none of them has handled its publicity with the flair of Longleat and Woburn. And not even these two enterprises, inventive as they are, have brought to their presentation the business acumen that Lord Montagu and his staff have applied to Beaulieu.

Beaulieu today is a complex that unashamedly sets out to make a profit from providing family entertainment, and to plough this back into the estate. In many respects its management is as up-to-date as any. From a professional standpoint, Lord Montagu is ahead of his rivals not only in promotion to bring the public in, but also in the services available once the visitor has paid to enter. The presentation of the 'Beaulieu Museum Complex' owes much to techniques refined in efficiency-conscious Disneyland, with similarities in traffic flow, reception, ticketing, entry – Lord Montagu has made a business of his inheritance. Whereas Lord Bath was – and remains – essentially an amateur, Lord Montagu is a professional. Henry Bath put his reputation on the line in taking the great gamble in 1949 (and by great good fortune won his bet and emerged as a natural publicist). However, Edward Montagu, opening three years later, had already gained a track record with the publicity machine. He knew how to tune it and make it sing sweetly. The tools he selected to bring financial viability to Beaulieu were those used by any successful, commercial company. Of course he took risks. Of course he worked extremely hard. And of course his approach was creative and inventive. The real inventiveness which Lord Montagu brought to bear was in grafting 20th-century show business and marketing skills onto the largely amateur practice of opening to the public.

'I already had some experience in public relations,' he explains, 'when I succeeded to the estate in 1951. I found then that around £150,000 was needed just to keep it in good shape. To my dismay I also discovered that its annual expendable income was less than £1,500. But I had been brought up to believe that Beaulieu was the most important thing in my life. Whatever else I did, the property – house, estate, and the people who lived on it – had to be secured for the future. Quite clearly, however, there was not much money around. Eventually 15 per cent of the estate was sold, and the capital used for improvements. That reduced the place to 8,000 acres, which was about its original size at the beginning of the 13th century.'

Few estates dating from the early Middle Ages have survived as intact as Beaulieu. Where Hampshire touches the Solent, split by the salt of Southampton Water, the map's grey hatchings tell of bricks and mortar hugging the eastern shoreline. To the west, by contrast, much is enticingly green, and for reasons that go back to the Norman kings. For this is the New Forest, a tract of country 'afforested' by William I since he

Lord Montagu's vineyard, whose rosé wine is especially worth remembering when dining at his Master Builder's House Hotel at Buckler's Hard.

placed it under Forest Law to preserve its animals for the royal chase. The laws he invoked, which had operated in Saxon England, were enforced by the powerful Forest Courts and became increasingly strengthened under the Normans. Settlements and enclosures were actively discouraged in this personal hunting ground of the monarch. One reason why the area is still comparatively unpeopled more than 900 years later, is the zealous professionalism brought to the Forest's jurisdiction by those who succeeded its royal proprietors.

Beaulieu straddles the Beaulieu River – the village on one side, house and Abbey on the other. By this point, the river has already wandered ten miles or more through the New Forest from north of Lyndhurst. From Beaulieu south to the Solent, however, the landscape flattens, the river broadens and assumes a different character. Trees hold the banks with grey contorted roots. Beds of reeds bend, hissing in the wind, and the water coils luxuriantly in its serpentine channel for a final five miles to the bar at its mouth.

At the highest navigable point, at the river's tidal head, a Cistercian abbot and 30 monks established their Abbey in 1204. Even more so than today, the site at that time would have had a lonely, haunting beauty. From the fine oak woods of the higher ground, and areas supporting heath and scrub, a visitor in the 13th century would approach the tidal stretch across saltmarsh and mudflats under wide pale skies loud with the cries of wildfowl and waders. It was this emptiness, though, that would have been welcomed by the Cistercians. It is known that a substantial hunting lodge belonging to the king already existed on the spot and the name of the place – Bellus Locus Regis or 'the king's beautiful place' – was rendered quite literally from Latin into the monks' own tongue as Beaulieu. If it seems incongruous that a substantial religious house should be permitted to take root in the heart of the king's private hunting ground, it comes as an even greater suprise to learn that its foundation was at the express wish of 'bad' King John. When we discover, moreover, that this same king had already granted these Cistercians the manor of Farringdon, in Oxfordshire, and that by charter he now handed them Beaulieu, together with the bed of the river to its outflow in the Solent and nearly 8,000 acres of surrounding land, then two alternatives have to be considered. The first is that King John has been the victim of character assassination and there has been a cover-up on his charity; the second that his motives for founding the Abbey were frankly too obscure to understand at the time and no-one has ever troubled to explain them since.

'Saltmarsh and mudflats under wide pale skies' where the Beaulieu river wanders south to join the Solent.

Ancient and modern: the Monorail frames Beaulieu's medieval abbey.

'History,' observes Lord Montagu, 'has not exactly painted King John as a man devoted to good or saintly works. Yet the Abbey at Beaulieu was certainly his protegé, his own – if his only – religious foundation. And he clearly intended it to survive and succeed.'

King John sanctioned grants towards the Abbey's building costs to the tune of the then enormous total of £1,600 (say £½ million today). How, then, are the King's actions to be explained? Could they represent some sudden altruism, an uncharacteristic burst of generosity? Was there some hidden political motive? Or some Machiavellian and deep-laid financial advantage? Alternatively, of course, the legend may be true. This tells of John's nightmare leading to remorse and terror following a tantrum in which he had ordered his mounted servants to ride down a deputation of Cistercian abbots.

The story certainly tallies with historical records. A dispute about money which the King was trying to extract from the Order is recorded for around the year 1200. The matter came to a head during a Parliament held at Lincoln, and it led to a period of disfavour on the king's part and of resentment on the part of the monks. Since it is also known that the situation was resolved through the diplomacy of the Archbishop of Canterbury, it may be conjectured that the king's sponsorship of Beaulieu formed part of the Archbishop's reconciliation package. It is some comfort, too, to have it confirmed that even Norman kings could not trample the clergy beneath their hooves and get away without any penalty whatever.

At the same time it is worth considering the strategic siting of King John's hunting lodge. That Beaulieu offered such easy access to the Solent can surely be no coincidence. Further, the Pipe Rolls tell us that as recently as 1199 it had been thoroughly done up at considerable cost. So the king was already concentrating on this property both financially and practically. Perhaps, with France increasingly on his mind, he was toying with an idea of a naval base on the Beaulieu, or of using it as a springboard to his Duchy over the water. What better, then, than to have it secured by a community already indebted to his patronage – a community, moreover, whose loyalty would be upheld by their shrewd and ambitious abbot? It would be churlish to put it down to mere coincidence that Beaulieu's abbot was, in fact, just such a man. Experienced, urbane, a man of substance and distinction, he was more than once called upon to serve on government commissions and to undertake diplomatic missions both at home and overseas.

Oblivious, meanwhile, of the clouded ambitions of kings, the monks of Beaulieu set about organizing their estate. Until their arrival, such

Working forestry, a feature of the estate since the monks arrived in the 13th century.

management as there had been was in the interests of game conservancy rather than for profit from timber and agriculture but the monks were out to maximize income. They concentrated the Abbey's forestry operations in the areas embracing Hartford and Otterwood, which served also as their abbot's hunting preserve. Sheep husbandry was centred on their holding named Begerie, cattle on the farm called Beufre. These simple Norman names are still used today to describe the farms on the same sites. About 4,000 sheep were kept, for their fleeces rather than meat, English wool being the most coveted in Europe and providing the bulk of the national income. The Abbey of Beaulieu, of course, was doubly fortunate. It was exempt from the New Forest's restrictions and penalties, so almost unlimited pasturage was available.

Under Henry III, son of King John, more land was made over to the Abbey. Outlying properties, managed as granges, were worked by what might be termed 'associate' monks called lay brothers. Mostly landless and illiterate, these would normally gravitate to the cooperative security of a monastic set-up later in life as the choir monks. Over the years, the fully-fledged monks, their working abilities hampered by the routine of their calling, came increasingly to depend on their lay brothers' input. By the turn of the 13th century, the Beaulieu work force had risen from 30 to around 200. During the golden years, the Abbey lay brothers were engaged in running not only Beaulieu's own massive wool warehouse in Southampton but its tannery producing hides, its own brewhouse, a small fleet of ships berthed on the Beaulieu river, its tide mill, a fishing business for local catches – plus even a herring salting enterprise on the river Yare in Norfolk. The wealth from its dependent manors (some as far afield as Cornwall) would be stacked in massive storehouses such as the Great Coxwell tithe barn on the Farringdon estate which King John had presented to the founding abbot. This cathedral among barns with its magnificent roof timbers still exists, in the ownership of the National Trust. More than 50 yards long, it stored in its cavernous interior one-tenth of the corn produced by Beaulieu's manorial tenants in Oxfordshire.

But like most lords of the manor across the country, Beaulieu and other abbeys saw their workforce – or at any rate their free labour – decline sharply from the 14th century. Hitherto the land tenure system in England had ensured that the serfs put in work on their lord's demesne on pre-arranged work-days. Feudalism imposed from above, however, could not be sustained once the peasants had a taste of the monetary system. Three factors speeded the move towards this. The first had to do with labour efficiency. Prescribed work days, obliging a peasant to leave his own field strip to fulfil a resented obligation on his master's home farm, resulted not only in, at the best, grudging labour but a lack of continuity on the manor farm. So some estates, as early as the 12th century, had moved into accepting cash rents from their peasants in lieu of labour and paying them cash in return for regular work. The second factor tied in with the first. This was that money became accessible to the humblest in the land once he had broken into the wool business. And when a peasant's flock gave him coin in the hand, he found the wherewithal to commute his forced services for money.

The third factor was the Black Death. It is ironic that the passport offered the serfs to escape from their former state and their emergence as free and sometimes yeoman farmers, was a by-product of the same plague which reduced their ranks by a third or, in some places, as much as a half. But in the previous century conditions had favoured the lords of the manor. A steep rise in population had led to increasing pressures on land, enabling landowners to turn the screws when negotiating tenure agreements with starving families. Their agents were ruthless on allocating fieldwork. But the aftermath of the Black Death of 1348–49 gave the whip-hand to the peasants. Those who survived took in hand the neglected field strips of their neighbours who had died. Furthermore, nearly twice as much coinage was suddenly in circulation. Labour shortages hit the big estates to tilt the bargaining advantage from employer to employee.

Throughout England at this time the lay brothers on whom the system depended came to realize that their labour had a market value. Becoming increasingly independent and difficult to control, they steadily slipped the ties of monastic security for the challenge of private enterprise. Around 140 lay brothers had worked for Beaulieu in 1270. But 1390 a mere 30 remained. During the same period the village beyond the Abbey walls began to grow. Money was changing hands; wages were paid for well-earned labour. By the 15th century, the Abbey's *Domus* – the massive communal centre that housed the lay brothers – was converted into accommodation for visiting worthies. Now, too, the monetary system affected the outlying granges, the Abbey being obliged to lease them to private individuals.

This, then, was the situation in the 1530s when Henry VIII set about dismantling the monasteries. The king's Commissioners were able in all honesty to report that at Beaulieu, as elsewhere, the strict Cistercian code had long been thrown to the winds. The first of their vows of poverty, chastity and silence had clearly been doomed on the collapse of the lay brother system. The early 16th century was the day of the money men. Hard-faced accountants, lawyers, receivers and stewards had set up offices, even living quarters, within the Abbey precincts. These agents were hired professionals, brought in to handle the Abbey's commercial business for the mutual enrichment of both parties, and the findings of the Commissioners furnished the king with the justification for the policies he was bent on pursuing. In April 1538 Henry VIII received from its abbot the formal surrender of the Abbey of Beaulieu.

'Within three months,' says Lord Montagu, 'the property changed hands. 10,000 acres and – almost uniquely – the bed of the river which King John had granted – the 'whole close of Beaulieu' indeed – went in July 1538 to Sir Thomas Wriothesley for £1,350-3s-8d.'

Lord Montagu of Beaulieu is a direct descendant of Wriothesley, the future Lord Chancellor and 1st Earl of Southampton. He is thus the inheritor of an estate that was put together within 150 years of the Conquest. Apart from during those three short months, Beaulieu can be said to have only had two owners. From the 13th to the 16th century it belonged to the Cistercians; and from the 16th to the 20th century it has swung around within the same ramificatious family, coming finally to rest with the Montagu-Douglas-Scotts when it passed by marriage to the Duke of Buccleuch.

The switch from the Wriothesleys to the Scotts was by way of the marriages of three heiresses in four generations. This first was Elizabeth, daughter of the fourth Earl of Southampton, who brought the estate to her husband the first Duke of Montagu; the next was Mary, the second Duke's daughter, who married the fourth Earl of Cardigan; the third was another Elizabeth, this couple's daughter, through whom Beaulieu passed to her husband, the third Duke of Buccleuch.

Lord Monagu's great-grandfather, the fifth Duke of Buccleuch, was known as the Uncrowned King of Scotland. One of the richest and most powerful families north of the Border, and among the greatest land-owners in Britain, the Buccleuchs had never used Beaulieu as a permanent home. But this was to change from 1867 when the Duke gave the place to his second son as a wedding present. Lord Henry Scott (or Montagu-Douglas-Scott) moved in, and he made the former Abbey gatehouse his family home. Indeed, the title he later chose reflected how deeply he was involved with the property. He became the first Lord Montagu of Beaulieu. Needing a bigger house in the 1870s, Henry Scott considerably extended the building, one of the few left standing from pre-Reformation days. It was this house – part medieval, part Victorian, and known as Palace House – which his grandson, the third Lord Montagu of Beaulieu, opened to the public in 1952.

'My father died in 1929,' Edward Montagu explains, 'when I was little

*Lord Montagu of Beaulieu – England's most professional presenter
of the stately home, outside Palace House at Beaulieu.*

The abbey ruins have been open to visitors since the 1890s.

more than a baby. His idea was that I should get my education behind me before being saddled with the responsibilities of Beaulieu. So by the time I did succeed, when I reached 25 years of age, I had done my National Service and finished with university and had spent some time working in public relations. The latter was to prove extremely useful.'

At the time, there were principal attractions to draw visitors to Beaulieu. The first was Palace House with its garden, set beside the mill pool on the river. Although a largish and comfortable country house, it was not particularly grand, and its contents were by no means all of museum quality. To the art-historian with an eye for antiquity it had its interesting features. But a lot of reorganization and 'packaging' would be needed if the general public was to get its money's worth. The second element comprised the vestiges of Beaulieu Abbey that had survived the asset-stripping of Sir Thomas Wriothesley. On acquiring the estate, Wriothesley had demolished the Abbey church and most of the larger buildings and contributed their stone and the lead from their roofs to Hurst Castle and Calshot Castle, the new gun-forts which Henry VIII was busy constructing nearby. But the *Domus* was still standing, together with parts of the cloister, a magnificent Gothic doorway through which the choir monks entered the Abbey, and the steps that mounted to their dormitory – enough, that is, to enable the place to be brought alive with a little imagination, and to hint at the Abbey's former grandeur.

The third element which the public had long enjoyed lay a couple of miles down the Beaulieu River. This was the 18th-century village of Buckler's Hard with its own historic associations. The brain-child in 1724 of John, second Duke of Montagu, Buckler's Hard had been intended to become a free port. It was to have handled sugar from the West Indian islands of St Lucia and St Vincent, where the Duke was planning to create plantations. George I granted Montagu the Governorship of these islands, and he encouraged Montagu's ambitions to annex them for Britain. The plan was scuppered by the French however, who put a larger force on St Lucia than Montagu's colonists could muster, thus snatching the prize from under his nose.

Instead, this tiny riverside community became a flourishing shipbuilding centre under the name of Buckler's Hard. Between 1745 and 1822 it launched over 50 ships for the Royal Navy, and a number of merchantmen. Most of the ships were built by master shipbuilder Henry Adams and the two sons who took over from him. A century and a half later Lord Montagu was carefully to convert a former inn on the site and create in it a museum of local history. With its accent on ships and shipbuilding, this was formally opened by Earl Mountbatten in 1963. Linked to the main

*Daily life in one of the Buckler's Hard cottages is vividly recalled
by models and authentic furnishings.*

museum, a series of 18th-century interiors depicts everyday life in the years when the navy came to the Adams family on the Beaulieu River for its fighting ships.

Essentially, the village comprises an 80ft-wide gravel street flanked by a dozen or so pink brick cottages. In 1952 these were in various states of disrepair. But their setting was so breath-taking above the wide expanse of water, deep woods beyond over the serene Beaulieu estuary, the simplicity of the village contrasting with the yachts on the river, that weekends and Bank Holidays saw visitors flocking to Buckler's Hard. Their very numbers soon created problems of congestion. In the 1960s, therefore, Lord Montagu constructed new car parks out of sight, and he built a new yacht harbour upstream with its own access road. These moves, among others, relieved the pressure of cars. His second conservation phase, announced in 1980, resulted in the exterior of the cottages being restored to their late 18th-century appearance, while internal renovation helped to revitalize the community. At the same time, a handful of cottages were appropriately furnished to recreate daily life in the 18th century and were inhabited by period models, to show how life was lived in them in their shipbuilding days.

But between opening the doors of Palace House and the emergence of Buckler's Hard as a living museum, Lord Montagu made his mark by creating a museum of a very different kind.

Since Palace House, although a comfortable country house with historic associations, was not in the Chatsworth league as a depository of world-class art treasures, Edward concentrated first on the portraits. In the rooms which he planned to put on view he hung pictures relating to the history of Beaulieu or the nation. Next, with the Coronation approaching, he put together a display relating to former coronations, while another room was devoted to Buckler's Hard. Here he displayed old maps and naval relics, scale models of men-of-war, a portrait of John, Duke of Montagu, and so on. From the start, however, it was plain to Edward that to be really successful he would have to come up with some additional and really strong attraction. At the same time he wished to establish a feature that would serve as a memorial to his father. When the answer came, he saw that it had been staring him in the face. The answer was a motor museum.

Lord Montagu's father had been one of the great pioneers of modern motoring. He was the first Englishman to race a British car on the Continent. As an MP he had introduced and steered through the 1903 Motor Car Bill. He was also the founder and long-time editor of one of Britain's earliest car magazines – *Car Illustrated*. 'More important at the

Buckler's Hard.

'. . . one car doesn't make a museum'.

The world's largest and most exciting motor museum.

time,' recalls his son, 'his 1903 De Dion Bouton was still at Beaulieu. I got it out and had it completely refurbished.

One car, however, does not make a museum. So Edward started asking around. Exhibits were sold, loaned and given to Beaulieu. Many came from motor manufacturers who were by no means unaware of the publicity potential. On the morning of 6th April 1952 five veteran cars, in the pink of condition, were waiting like starlets for the cameras to roll, hidden by screens in the entrance hall. But Edward contrived to keep them a secret. The celebration – ostensibly – was for the first public opening of Palace House. People entered by a side door. Naturally, the press was well represented, and they trooped into the Picture Gallery in the former Library. 'At that point,' remembers Edward, 'I made a short introductory announcement, concluding by introducing England's first motor museum since Edmund Dangerfield's 1912 attempt at the Crystal Palace. Everyone headed for the hall. We had opened the doors at 10.00, and I remember how I had promised my friends that if 100 visitors had showed up by 6.00 we'd have champagne at dinner. Who was the luckiest – my guests or me? By twelve noon the hundredth visitor paid his entrance fee. I opened the first bottle before one'

The Montagu Motor Museum had arrived. The *Daily Mail*'s announcement the following morning – 'Old Crocks are now on show in King John's Abbey' – was no prophesy of a nine-day wonder. Steadily, and with increasing momentum, vintage and veteran vehicles found their way to Beaulieu. In 1956, the Motor Museum moved to occupy two wooden buildings in the garden, and it was not long before more sophisticated housing and display were called for. Accordingly, in April 1959, a greatly enlarged Montagu Motor Museum was opened by Lord Brabazon of Tara. The following year saw the birth of the Transport Library in response to a growing public interest. It also brought the first wedding couple to hire a car from the museum, and Beaulieu's first veteran and vintage car auction. Nobody by this time talked of old crocks. Edward Montagu's achievement had coincided with, and fostered, an upsurge of interest in early motoring history. His collection, meanwhile, was so gaining in numbers and importance that it was decided to form a special body to administer the venture. In this way the National Motor Museum was conceived. In December 1970, the museum's foundation stone was laid, and in July 1972 it was opened by the Duke of Kent.

The museum is owned by the National Motor Museum Trust, a charitable foundation whose trustees are quite separate from Montagu Ventures Limited. The Trust's offices near the museum (which was named the John Montagu Building after Edward's father) house the

Easter visitors to the National Motor Museum;
the Brabazon complex is on the left.

curator, administrator, the keeper of exhibits, and the museum's education and research officer. Also housed here are the museum's library and photographic library, open to everyone 365 days a year. The photographic library's facility is complete with darkrooms, and sound and film archives

Beaulieu is a considerable business enterprise. Half a dozen inter-relating organizations operate under the chairmanship of Lord Montagu. Each organization is further divided into specialist departments. A permanent staff of 300 keeps the machinery running, and in the busy summer months this is increased by half as much again to a total of about 450. Fundamentally, the aim of the enterprise is to ensure the estate's continued existence as an entity in family ownership. At the same time it seeks to enhance the qualities of the estate and to make appropriate parts of it available for public enjoyment.

The key organization within the whole is Montagu Ventures Limited, around which the others are grouped. The specific objectives of Montagu Ventures, summarized in the Beaulieu Staff Handbook, are: 'To provide public access to sites suitable for leisure and recreational activities at Beaulieu and Buckler's Hard, while protecting more sensitive areas of the estate; to manage leisure facilities at Beaulieu and Buckler's Hard including Palace House and gardens, Beaulieu Abbey, the National Motor Museum, and at Buckler's Hard the village, historic cottages and Maritime Museum; to market these facilities to attract the maximum number of visitors which may be accommodated without detriment to either the physical environment or visitor enjoyment; to apply income from leisure activities to either the improvement of visitor services and facilities or the restoration and conservation of heritage buildings and landscape within the boundaries of the estate.'

Under the Montagu Ventures umbrella comes also what are termed 'visitor services' and 'special features'. The former embrace things which are ancilliary to the main attractions yet make a visit more enjoyable. These have the ring of an extract from a demented foreign phrase-book: 'Accommodation, Bank, Cameras & Film, Cigarette Machines, Credit Cards, Education, First Aid . . . Found Articles, Lost Articles, Lost Children . . . Motor Museum Library . . . Picnic Facilities, Post Office & Stamps, Taxis, Telephones, Toilets, Travellers' Cheques . . .'. Then the 'special features,' too, together with 'special events', might suggest that the organization has wandered somewhat from just providing a pleasant day out for the country house visitor. Challenging both language and imagination, here are grouped the Monorail, the Transporama, the Veteran Bus, Veteran Car Ride, Mini Cars and Bikes, and the Radio Cars.

And there is 'Wheels' – the latest million-pound attraction which whisks the visitor on a journey through motoring history in a section of the Motor Museum.

Besides these, there is the Model Railway run by a concessionaire, while the Events department liaises with outsiders mounting activities. It oversees, for example, a ticket check at the entrance to the Rally Field, and administers the annual 'Boatjumble' and 'Autojumble'.

Visitor income is earned by Montagu Ventures, as it is also by the Catering department. This is operated by a division of Allied-Lyons. There are four main catering points – a free-flow cafeteria in the Brabazon complex, the Master Builder's House Hotel and the Mulberry Cafeteria at Buckler's Hard, and the Domus Banqueting Hall where, upstairs in the lay brothers' 14th-century building, 'authentic' medieval banquets are a regular weekly feature. At the height of the season, as many as 3,000 ice-creams are served a day in the Brabazon alone.

Another unit in the organization, Beaulieu River Management, manages the river as a navigable waterway, controlling yachting activity to preserve the visual amenity of the estuary, and ensuring the long-term conservation of fish and shell-fish stocks. It also administers the marina, the boat moorings and its own cruise boat for visitors. Meanwhile, the Beaulieu Estate has responsibility for land management, property, farms and forestry, and for the river itself as opposed to its leisure activities. Finally, and dependant from the Estate department, there is the Countryside Education Trust. This is concerned with educational access to the estate's countryside areas and with the conservation of the estate's ecological and architectural features. The relationship between each of these departments is balanced through a system of lease and rent. Beaulieu River Management, for example, pays rent to the Estate in return for its lease. In this way all the activities of the complex are mutually supporting: each contributes to and draws upon Montagu Ventures Limited which in turn ensures the future of the property as a whole and the interests of those who work within it. 'How could life at Beaulieu be dull,' asks Ken Robinson, Managing Director of Montagu Ventures, 'when among its staff are monorail drivers, accountants, artists, photographers, teachers, gardeners, chefs, vehicle engineers, carpenters, archivists, reception hostesses, shop assistants, woodsmen – and a harbour master?'

More than 35 years have passed since Edward Montagu re-hung family portraits in a couple of rooms and offered a tea shop in a cellar with seating for 40. Now the Beaulieu Organization is big business. It is tempting to disparage the commercialism of the '80s which succeeds the brave new world of the early '50s, to feel that the weasels have taken over Toad Hall.

*Harbour Master Bill Grindey, but one of a permanent staff numbering 300,
ensures that 'life is never dull' at Buckler's Hard.*

By selecting a Director for his Buckler's Hard museum who was already an established model maker, Edward Montagu was able to enthuse the public with the most perfect scale models of 18th-century fighting ships.

*Brian Moase, Lord Montagu's gamekeeper, mastermind
of four productive shoots.*

On the credit side, however, the museums are not merely good but very good. Large numbers of people derive positive pleasure from visiting and revisiting Beaulieu. The river is managed admirably for the enjoyment of yachtsmen and day visitors and also for the long-term health of the environment. And – as was Edward Montagu's intention in the first place – the estate has not only survived but continues to prosper. Today it is thriving with 20 farms leased to tenants, forestry in hand, four productive shoots giving Edward his shooting, a five-acre vineyard dating from the 'fifties, and some of the finest fishing in the south. Upstream of the bridge is a run of sea trout, while downstream the estate still maintains the medieval tradition of seine netting for mullet and bass on alternate Fridays in the season.

Beaulieu is as buoyant today as at any time in the seven and a half centuries it has existed as anything more than a hunting preserve. There are its farms and two villages, its houses, shops, and a couple of garages, and the ancient tide-mill currently scheduled for restoration and to be added to the attractions for visitors. Edward's son, Ralph Montagu, who lives at Palace House, is deeply involved in the well-being of the estate and takes a keen interest in all its activities from farming and forestry to the public attractions.

'Anyone who has inherited an important house and estate has in these times to adapt. He can't possibly keep going on agricultural rents in the way that was accepted in former centuries. Indeed,' adds Lord Montagu with a gesture that embraces the Motor Museum and Beaulieu's many other visitor attractions, 'he will certainly have to adopt a progressive and commercial attitude if the estate and its community is to survive.'